TOMAS TRANSTRÖMER
SELECTED POEMS
1954–1986

TOMAS TRANSTRÖMER SELECTED POEMS 1954–1986

TRANSLATED BY
ROBERT BLY, ROBIN FULTON,
MAY SWENSON, SAMUEL CHARTERS,
JOHN F. DEANE, JOANNA BANKIER,
ERIC SELLIN, AND OTHERS

EDITED BY
ROBERT HASS

ecco

An Imprint of HarperCollinsPublishers

Introduction copyright © 1987 by Robert Hass

The editor would like to thank Joanna Bankier for her generous and indispensable help and Kristin Hass for her editorial labors.

Published by The Ecco Press in 1987
100 West Broad Street, Hopewell, New Jersey 08525
Published simultaneously in Canada by
Penguin Books Canada Ltd., Ontario

Printed in the United States of America

Publication of this book was made possible in part by a grant from the National Endowment for the Arts.

Library of Congress Cataloging in Publication Data
    Tranströmer, Tomas, 1931–
    Tomas Tranströmer: selected poems, 1954–1986.

    Translated from Swedish.
    1. Tranströmer, Tomas, 1931–   —Translations, English.
I. Bly, Robert. II. Hass, Robert. III. Title.
PT9876.3.R3A23 1987   839.7'174   86-24257
ISBN 0-88001-105-X
ISBN 0-88001-113-0 (paper)

ACKNOWLEDGMENTS

Joanna Bankier: "How-Things-Hang-Together," "Through the Forest," "November Luster of Precious Furs," and "Summer Meadow" are copyright © 1987 by Joanna Bankier. "Black Postcards" appeared in *The Threepenny Review* and is copyright © 1986 by Joanna Bankier.

Robert Bly: "Track," "After the Attack," "The Couple," "Lamento," "Allegro," "Nocturne," "From an African Diary (1963)," "After a Death," "Out in the Open," "Breathing Space July," "Outskirts," "The Open Window," "Standing Up," "Guard Duty," "Further In," "Elegy," "Seeing Through the Ground," and "The Scattered Congregation" are copyright © 1975 by Robert Bly and are reprinted, sometimes in slightly revised form, from *Friends, You Drank Some*

Page 189 constitutes an extension of this page

CONTENTS

3. FROM THE HALF-FINISHED HEAVEN (1962)

4. FROM BELLS AND TRACKS (1966)

5. SEEING IN THE DARK (1970)

6. PATHS (1973)

INTRODUCTION

Tomas Tranströmer published his first book of poems—the stunning *17 Dikter*—in 1954 when he was twenty-three years old. Eight volumes have followed, each rather brief and beautifully shaped. By 1966 a first selection of his work translated by Eric Sellin had appeared in the *New Directions Annual No. 19.* Since then he has been translated into English more regularly than any European poet of the postwar generation. Robert Bly printed his *Twenty Poems of Tomas Tranströmer* in 1971. May Swenson, in collaboration with Leif Sjoberg, published a selected poems, *Windows and Stones,* in 1972. Three of the individual Swedish volumes have been translated complete and published in the United States: Bly's *Night Vision* in 1972 and his *Truth-Barriers* in 1981, and Samuel Charters's translation of the long poem *Baltics* in 1975. A version of Tranströmer's most recent book, *The Wild Market Square,* appeared in Dublin in 1985, translated by John F. Deane. The Scotch poet Robin Fulton, in the meantime, had published a *Selected Poems* in the Penguin European Poets series in 1972. Robert Bly published an enlarged selection of his translations in 1975 and Fulton's volume, also enlarged, was published in the United States in 1979. And other translators have worked on various individual poems.

The intention of the present volume is to draw the best of this work together in a single book. The idea was Daniel Halpern's. Mr. Tranströmer thought that an American poet, reading the translations simply with an eye to what read well in English, might make an interesting editor. I undertook the job, qualified by my ignorance of Swedish. It turned out to be a little less simple than it might have seemed. There were often three or four translations of a poem available, each with its own virtue. Reading and comparing the translation often raised questions of tone and of literal accuracy. In the end I went through the poems in Swedish with the extremely generous assistance of Joanna Bankier, herself a translator and Tranströmer scholar. I made some suggestions for revision to the individual translators and they, given the opportunity to reprint their work, found their own reasons to revise—translating being a fiddler's task as editing is a meddler's.

The result of this collaboration is the present book, virtually a new and complete poems in English translation. I had to omit from the two Swedish volumes, the Bonniers *Collected Poems* of 1982 and *Det Vilda Torget* of 1983 only seven or eight poems, which could not somehow be gotten into effective English, and regretted the loss of only one, the rich blank verse "Sang" from *17 Dikter,* which needed to be in fairly regular blank verse in English and has so far resisted the metamorphosis. I have included several poems about which their author has come to have doubts—or stronger feelings—because they seemed to belong to the record being made. I was somewhat worried that a book like this, containing so many voices, might suffer from the loss of a sense of unity in its tone. But it is my impression that Tranströmer's voice, spare and clear, and the undistractable clarity and intensity of his vision have carried those small differences in tone.

So, this book is also the record of the devotion of a number of people to a remarkable body of poetry. I want to thank Robert Bly, Robin Fulton, Samuel Charters, and May Swenson for their responsiveness and Robert Bly for sharing his vivid sense of the music of Tranströmer's verse. Special thanks are due to Leif Sjoberg who supplied May Swenson with word for word translations of the poems, to supplement her childhood Swedish, when she was working on *Windows and Stones,* and consulted with her on both the original work and on the recent revisions. Joanna Bankier was unstinting, generous both in her knowledge of the poetry and in her literary judgment. And I want to thank Kristin Hass for her editorial labors.

ROBERT HASS

I

PRELUDE

Awakening is a parachute jump from the dream.
Freed from the choking vortex, the diver
sinks towards the green map of morning.
Things magnify. He sees, from the fluttering lark's
position, huge tree-root systems
like branchings of subterranean chandeliers. Above ground,
in tropical flood, earth's greenery
stands with lifted arms, as if listening
to the beat of invisible pistons. And he
sinks towards summer, is lowered
into its dazzling crater, lowered
between fissures of moist green eons
trembling under the sun's turbine. Then halts
the downward dive through time's eyeblink, the wingspread
becomes an osprey's glide over streaming water.
Bronze Age trumpets:
their outlaw tune
hangs motionless over the void.

In the day's first hours consciousness can own the world
like a hand enclosing a sun-warm stone.
The skydiver stands under the tree.
With the plunge through death's vortex
will light's great chute spread over his head?

AUTUMN IN THE SKERRIES

Storm

Suddenly, out walking, he meets the giant
oak, like an ancient petrified elk, with
mile-wide crown in front of September's sea,
    the dusk-green fortress.

Storm from the north. When rowanberry
clusters ripen. Awake in the dark, he hears
constellations stamping in their stalls, high
    over the oak tree.

Evening-Morning

The moon's mast has rotted and the sail shriveled.
A gull soars drunkenly over the sea.
The jetty's thick quadrangle is charred. Brush
    bends low in the dusk.

Out on the doorstep. Daybreak slams and slams in
the sea's gray stone gateway, and the sun flashes
close to the world. Half-choked summer gods
    fumble in sea mist.

Ostinato

Under the buzzard's circling dot of stillness
the waves race roaring into the light,
chewing on their bridles of seaweed, snorting
    froth across the shore.

The earth is blind in darkness where the bats
take bearings. The buzzard stops and becomes a star.
The waves race roaring forth and snort
              froth across the shore.

FIVE STANZAS TO THOREAU

One more has fled the heavy city,
its ring of starved stones. Clear and salty are
the waters that immerse all
                  rebels' heads.

In a lazy spiral silence ascends
from earth's navel, takes root here, and grows
a thick crown of leaves to dapple
                  the sun-warm stairway.

.

Absently the foot kicks a mushroom. A thundercloud
swells on the horizon. Like trumpets
the trees' twisted roots vibrate, the leaves
                  flutter apart startled.

Autumn's wild passing is a flimsy cape,
the folds blowing until, out of frost and ash,
a flock of calm days comes again, to bathe
                  claws in the spring.

.

No one believes it, that you have seen a geyser,
fled the stagnant well like Thoreau, and that you know
how to vanish deep into your own greenwood,
                  crafty and hopeful.

GOGOL

Jacket worn and shabby like a pack of wolves.
Face like a marble chip.
Sitting in a ring of his letters in the grove that sighs
of mocking and mistakes.
Yes, the heart is blown like paper through inhospitable
passages.

Now sunset steals like a fox across this land
setting the grass on fire in a moment.
The sky is filled with horns and hooves, and underneath
the calèche glides shadowy between my father's
illuminated estates.

St. Petersburg situated at the latitude of annihilation
(did you see the beauty in the leaning tower?)
and around iced-in city blocks the pauper in his overcoat,
still floating like a jellyfish.

And here, wrapped in fasts, the man who was surrounded by
                        hordes of laughter,
but they have long since departed for districts far above
                        the timberline.
Mankind's reeling tables.
Look outside, how the darkness sears a Milky Way of souls.
So mount your chariot of fire and leave the country!

SAILOR'S YARN

There are bare winter days when the sea is kin
to mountain country, crouching in gray plumage,
a brief minute blue, long hours with waves like pale
lynxes vainly seeking hold in the beach-gravel.

On such a day wrecks might come from the sea searching
for their owners, settling in the town's din, and drowned
crews blow landward, thinner than pipe-smoke.

(The real lynxes are in the north, with sharpened claws
and dreaming eyes. In the north, where day
lives in a mine both day and night.

Where the sole survivor may sit
at the borealis stove and listen
to the music of those frozen to death.)

STROPHE AND ANTISTROPHE

The outermost circle is the myth's. There the helmsman sinks upright
among glittering dorsals.
How far from us! When the day
lingers in a close and windless motion—
as the Congo's green shadow holds
the blue men in its vapor—
when all that driftwood piles up
along the heart's sluggish
winding river.

Suddenly a change: in under the firmament's repose
glide the tethered ones.
High in the stern, with hopeless
bearings, looms the hull of a dream, black
against the light-red coastal strip. Abandoned
the years fall, swiftly
and soundlessly—as the sled's shadow, doglike, large,
travels over the snow,
reaches the woods.

AGITATED
MEDITATION

A storm makes the vanes of the mill whiz around
in night's darknesss grinding nothing. —You
                  keep awake by the same logic.
The gray shark's belly is your faint lamp.

Vague memories sink to the ocean's floor
and stiffen there—unfamiliar statues. —Green
                  with algae is your crutch. Who
goes to sea comes back turned to stone.

STONES

Stones that we have thrown I hear
falling, glass-clear through the years. In the valley
fly the moment's chaotic
acts shrieking from
treetop to treetop. Made mute
in thinner air than that of the present, they glide
like swallows over mountain
and mountain, until they
reach the farthest plains
at the edges of existence. There fall
all our deeds
glass-clear
to no bottom
except within ourselves.

HOW-THINGS-
HANG-TOGETHER

See that gray tree. The heavens have run
through its fibers into the earth—
only a shriveled sky remains when
earth has had her fill. Stolen space
is twisted into a mesh of roots, twined
into greenery. Brief moments
of freedom rise out of us, whirl
through the Norns'* blood and beyond.

*In Norse mythology, the Fates.

MORNING AND ENTRANCE

The black-backed gull, the sun-skipper, steers his course.
Under him is wide water.
The world still sleeps like a
many-colored stone in the water.
Undeciphered day. Days—
like Aztec hieroglyphs!

The music. And I stand captive
in its Gobelin tapestry, with
upraised arms—like a figure
from primitive art.

THERE IS PEACE IN
THE SURGING BOW

On a winter morning you feel how this earth
plunges ahead. Against the house walls
an air current smacks
out of hiding.

Surrounded by movement: the tent of calm.
And the secret helm in the migrating flock.
Out of the winter gloom
a tremolo rises

from hidden instruments. It is like standing
under summer's high lime tree with the din
of ten thousand
insect wings above your head.

MIDNIGHT TURNING
POINT

Unmoving, the ant in the forest looks into
nothing. And nothing is heard but the ticking
of dark greenery, nightlong the murmur deep
                        in summer's chasm.

The spruce tree at point, like a clock's jagged
hand. The ant aglow in the mountain's shadow.
A bird screams! At last. Slowly the cloud cart
                        begins to roll.

ELEGY

At the starting point. Our spruce-clad coastline
is like a fallen dragon amidst haze
and fumes as in some marsh. A long way out
two steamships that call out dreamlike

within the mist. It is the lower world.
Unmoving woods, unmoving water surface
and stretching from the earth the orchid's hand.
Beyond this channel, on the other side

but in the same reflections hung, The Ship,
as weightlessly a cloud hangs in its space.
And around its stern the water's motionless,
lying in a calm. And still it storms!

and horizontally the ship's smoke blows—
the sun is shaken in its grip—and on
the face of one who boards the gale blows hard.
To make it to the larboard side of Death.

A sudden crosswind and the curtain flutters.
The silence ringing like an alarm clock.
A sudden crosswind and the curtain flutters.
Until a door's heard slamming in the distance

a long way off in another year.

·

O fields and woods, gray as the Bogman's* cloak!
The island floating darkly in the mist.

*One whose body, buried in ancient times, has been pre-
served owing to certain acids in the bog.

There is a silence when the radar turns
its circles upon circles in despair.

A crossroad is contained within a moment.
The music of what is distant streams and joins.
All grown together in a bushy tree.
Lost cities shining in its foliage.

From everywhere and nowhere it is playing
like crickets in the August dark. At night
the murdered traveler slumbers in the bog
    indriven like a timber beetle. Sap drives

his thoughts upward towards the stars. And deep
within the mountain: here is the bat's cave.
Here the years, the deeds are thickly hanging.
Here they sleep with tightly folded wings.

One day they will fly out. A swarm! (It looks,
afar, like smoke that leaves the cavern's mouth.)
But still the summerwinter sleep prevails.
Far off the water's hum. In the dark trees

a leaf turning.

•

A summer day the farmer's harrow sticks in
the dead man's bones and shreds of clothing.—After
the bog was drained he still was lying there
and in the light now stands and goes his way.

In every parish whirls the golden seed
around the old guilts. The armor-covered skull

in plowed-up fields. A hiker on the road
and the mountain trails him with its glance.

In every parish murmurs the marksman's pipe
when at the point of midnight wings are spread
and in its fall the past begins to grow
and darker than the meteor of the heart.

A turn away of spirit makes the writing
voracious. A flag begins to snap. The wings
around the prey. This proud journey! where
the albatross is aged into a cloud

inside Time's mouth. The culture is a whaling
station, where the stranger on a walk
among the playing children, the white houses,
is still with every breath he takes aware of

the murdered giant's presence.

·

Beyond, the black cock crooning of the spheres.
Guiltless in our shadow, Music, like
the fountain's water rising among beasts
artfully turned to stone around the spray.

With the violin bows now as a forest.
The violin bows like rigging in a downpour—
the cabin flung under the downpour's hooves—
a gyroscope's suspension is us, joy.

The world's calm is reflected in the evening,
when all the bows are lifted but don't move.

Immovable in mist the forest's trees
the watery tundra that reflects itself.

Music's mute half, like the smell of resin
from the thunder-injured spruce is here.
A summer underground for every man.
A shadow breaks free at the crossroads there

and following Bach's trumpet gallops off.
Now confidence is given out of grace.
To leave one's self-disguise there on the shore
where rollers break and ebb away, break

and ebb away.

EPILOGUE

December. Sweden is a hauled-up,
unrigged ship. Her masts stand stark
in the twilight. And twilight lasts longer
than day. The way here is stony:
daylight waits until noon
to reveal winter's coliseum,
lit by unreal clouds. Then suddenly
the white smoke climbs, twirling up
from the villages. Endlessly high, the clouds.
The sea gropes at heaven's root,
preoccupied and as if listening to something.
(Obscure journeys over the soul's dark,
half-averted the bird that could arouse
the sleeper with its chirp. Then the glass
is shifted, showing another time:
it is summer, the mountains bellow, swollen
with light, the brook carries the sun's glitter
in its transparent hand. . . . But all vanishes,
as when a filmstrip ends in the dark.)

Now the evening star burns through cloud.
Trees, fences and houses grow, grow larger
with the dark's soundless, steepening fall.
And under the star is outlined clear and clearer
the other, secret landscape that lives
the life of contour on night's X-ray plate.
A shadow draws its sled between the houses.
They wait.

      Six p.m., and the wind comes
springing with its noise along the street,
bursting into the dark like a pack of horsemen.
How the black disruption jangles, then dies down.
Dancing in place the houses stand, stricken

in this roar that is like a dream's. Gust
after gust sweeps over the bay, and out
to the open sea that casts itself into darkness.
Overhead the stars flash desperately,
switched on and off by racing clouds
which, only when they veil the light, reveal
their presence, like those clouds of the past
that wander through the soul. When I
pass the stable road I hear through the din
the sick horse's stamping from within.

The turning point in the storm is marked
by a broken gate that slams and slams, a lantern
that dangles from a hand, some beast that wails
afraid on the mountain. Retreating, thunder
tumbles over the cow-house roofs, twanging
telephone wires, forcing piercing whistles
from every tile and panel of the night,
and the helpless trees throw their branches.

A tune escapes from the bagpipes!
A bagpipe tune approaches, with its skirl
of freedom. A procession. A wood on the march!
A splashing around a prow, and darkness shifts,
land and water travel. And the dead
who have gone below deck, they are here,
with us on our way: a voyage, a crossing
that is not tempestuous but calm.

And the world constantly pitches its tent
anew. A summer day, and the wind takes hold
of the oak's tackle and hauls up the earth.
The water lily paddles on its hidden web foot

within the tarn's swift dark embrace.
A boulder is rolled away from the rim of space.

In summer twilight the islands rise
above the horizon. The old villages withdraw,
are on their way deeper into the woods,
with the season's wheel, the magpie's squawk.
When the year kicks off its boots
and the sun shinnies higher, trees take leaf,
are filled with wind and sail out freely.
At the mountain's foot the burnt and blasted pinewood,
but summer's long tepid surf will come,
drag through the fallen treetops slowly, rest
a moment, then sink lower, and recede,
leaving the leafless beach. And ultimately
God's soul is like the Nile: it overflows
and dries up, with a rhythm reckoned variously
in all the texts throughout the ages.

But He is also unchangeable,
and therefore seldom noticed here.
He crosses the path of march obliquely.

Like the vessel that passes through fog
without the fog observing a thing. Silence.
The lantern's slender beam is the signal.

2

SECRETS ON THE WAY
(1958)

SOLITARY
SWEDISH HOUSES

A tangle of black spruce
and smoking moonbeams.
Here's the croft lying low
and not a sign of life.

Till the morning dew murmurs
and an old man opens
—with a shaky hand—his window
and lets out an owl.

Further off, the new building
stands steaming
with the laundry butterfly
fluttering at the corner

in the middle of a dying wood
where the moldering reads
through spectacles of sap
the proceedings of the bark-drillers.

Summer with flaxen-haired rain
or one solitary thundercloud
above a barking dog.
The seed is kicking inside the earth.

Agitated voices, faces
fly in the telephone wires
on stunted rapid wings
across the moorland miles.

The house on an island in the river
brooding on its stony foundations.
Perpetual smoke—they're burning
the forest's secret papers.

The rain wheels in the sky.
The light coils in the river.
Houses on the slope supervise
the waterfall's white oxen.

Autumn with a gang of starlings
holding dawn in check.
The people move stiffly
in the lamplight's theatre.

Let them feel without alarm
the camouflaged wings
and God's energy
coiled up in the dark.

THE MAN WHO AWOKE
WITH SINGING OVER
THE ROOFS

Morning. May-rain. The city is still quiet
as a mountain hamlet. The streets quiet. And in
the sky a bluish-green aero-engine rumbles.—
                    The window is open.

The dream where the sleeper is lying prostrate
turns transparent. He stirs, begins
groping for attention's instruments—
                    almost in space.

WEATHER
PICTURE

The October sea glistens coldly
with its dorsal fin of mirages.

Nothing is left that remembers
the white dizziness of yacht races.

An amber glow over the village.
And all sounds in slow flight.

A dog's barking is a hieroglyph
painted in the air above the garden

where the yellow fruit outwits
the tree and drops of its own accord.

THE FOUR TEMPERAMENTS

The scanning eye turns sunbeams into billy clubs.
And in the evening: hubbub of a party downstairs
erupts like artificial flowers through the floor.

Crossed the plain. Darkness. Wagon apparently stuck.
An antibird shrieked in the star void.
An albino sun stood over the chopped dark sea.

·

A man like an uprooted tree with croaking leaves
and a lightning bolt at salute saw the whiff-of-wild-beast
sun shoot up through ruffling wings on the world's

rock island speeding behind flags of foam through night
and day, the white seafowl yelling
on deck and all with tickets to Chaos.

·

You've merely to shut your eyes to hear
the sea gulls tolling Sunday through the ocean's endless parish.
A guitar starts twanging in the thicket, a cloud shifts

idly as late-come spring's green sleigh
—the whinny of light between the shafts—
glides forward on the ice.

·

Woke up with my girlfriend's heels clicking in the dream
and, outside, a pair of snowdrifts like winter's lost gloves,
while handbills from the sun drifted down over the city.

Road never ends. Horizon races outward.
Birds shake in the tree. Dust whirls in the wheels.
All the rolling wheels that contradict death!

CAPRICHOS*

Twilight in Huelva: sooty palm trees
and fleet train whistles
like silver-haired bats.

The streets have been clogged with people.
A lady skimming through the crowd weighs carefully
the last ray of day on her eye's scale.

Office windows open. You can still hear
the tread of the horse inside.
The old horse with rubber-stamp hoofs.

Not until after midnight do the streets empty.
At last all the offices fill up with blue.

Up there in space:
trotting in silence, glistening and black,
unseen, unharnessed,
the rider thrown off:
a new constellation which I name "The Horse."

* Spanish, meaning "whims" or "fancies." Also, the title of
one of Goya's series of etchings.

SIESTA

Whitsuntide of the stones. And with crackling tongues . . .
The city suspended in the spaciousness of noon.
Interment in simmering light. The drum that drowns out
eternity's locked-up and pounding fists.

The eagle soars up and up over the sleepers.
A sleep where the mill wheel rumbles like thunder.
Thump of the horse with the blindfolded eyes.
Eternity's locked-up and pounding fists.

The sleepers are weights hung in the tyrant's clock.
The eagle drifts dead in the sun's white cataract.
And echoing through time—as in Lazarus' burial box—
eternity's locked-up and pounding fists.

IZMIR AT
THREE O'CLOCK

Just ahead in the almost empty street
two beggars, one without legs—
he's carried on the other one's back.

They stood—as on a midnight road an animal
stands blinded staring into the carlights—
for one moment before passing on

and scuttled across the street like boys
in a playground while the midday heat's
myriad of clocks ticked in space.

Blue flowed past on the waters, flickering.
Black crept and shrank, stared from stone.
White blew up to a storm in the eyes.

When three o'clock was tramped under hooves
and darkness pounded in the wall of light
the city lay crawling at the sea's door

gleaming in the vulture's telescopic sight.

SECRETS ON THE WAY

Daylight struck the face of a man who slept.
His dream was more vivid
but he did not wake.

Darkness struck the face of a man who walked
among the others in the sun's strong
impatient rays.

It was suddenly dark, like a downpour.
I stood in a room that contained every moment—
   a butterfly museum.

And the sun still as strong as before.
Its impatient brushes were painting the world.

TRACK

2 a.m.: moonlight. The train has stopped
out in a field. Far off sparks of light from a town,
flickering coldly on the horizon.

As when a man goes so deep into his dream
he will never remember that he was there
when he returns again to his room.

Or when a person goes so deep into a sickness
that his days all become some flickering sparks, a swarm,
feeble and cold on the horizon.

The train is entirely motionless.
2 o'clock: strong moonlight, few stars.

KYRIE

Sometimes my life opened its eyes in the dark.
A feeling as if crowds drew through the streets
in blindness and anxiety on the way towards a miracle,
while I invisibly remain standing.

As the child falls asleep in terror
listening to the heart's heavy tread.
Slowly, slowly until morning puts its rays in the locks
and the doors of darkness open.

A MAN FROM BENIN

(on a photograph of a fifteenth-century relief in bronze
from the Negro state of Benin, showing a Portuguese Jew)

When darkness fell I was still
but my shadow pounded
against the drumskin of hopelessness.
When the pounding began to ease
I saw the image of an image
of a man coming forward
in the emptiness, a page
lying open.
Like going past a house
long since abandoned
and someone appears at the window.
A stranger. He was the navigator.
He seemed to take notice.
Came nearer without a step.
In a hat which molded itself
imitating our hemisphere
with the brim at the equator.
The hair parted in two fins.
The beard hung curled
round his mouth like eloquence.
He held his right arm bent.
It was thin like a child's.
The falcon that should have had its place
on his arm grew out
from his features.
He was the ambassador.
Interrupted in the middle of a speech
which the silence continues
even more forcibly.
Three peoples were silent in him.
He was the image of three peoples.
A Jew from Portugal,
who sailed away with the others,
the drifting and the waiting ones,

the hunched-up flock
in the caravelle which was
their rocking wooden mother.
Landfall in a strange air
which made the atmosphere furry.
Observed in the marketplace
by the Negro cast-maker.
Long in his eyes' quarantine.
Reborn in the race of metal:
"I am come to meet him
who raises his lantern
to see himself in me."

BALAKIREV'S DREAM
(1905)

The black grand piano, the shiny spider,
trembled in the center of its net of music.

In the concert hall was conjured a land
where the stones were no heavier than dew.

But Balakirev* fell asleep during the music
and dreamed a dream about the Tsar's droshky.†

It wheeled out over the cobblestones
straight into the crow-cawing dark.

He sat alone in the carriage, looking out,
at the same time he ran beside it on the road.

He knew the journey had been long,
and his watch showed years, not hours.

There was a field where the plow lay
and the plow was a fallen bird.

There was an inlet where the vessel lay
icebound, lights out, the crew on deck.

The droshky raced out on the ice, the wheels
spun and spun with the sound of silk.

A minor man-of-war: *Sevastopol.*
He stood on board. The crew came forward.

*Milij Balakirev: Russian composer (1837–1910).
†Horse-drawn four-wheeled carriage used in Russia.

"Your life is spared if you can play."
They showed him a fabulous instrument.

It was like a tuba or a phonograph
or part of some unknown engine.

Helpless with fear, he understood: this
was the piston that drove the man-of-war.

He turned and faced the nearest sailor,
made desperate signs with his hands, and begged:

"Make the sign of the cross, make the cross!"
The sailor's eyes turned sad as a blind man's,

his arms stretched out, his head dropped forward—
there he hung as if nailed in the air.

The drums beat. The drums beat. Applause!
Balakirev woke up from his dream.

Wings of applause flapped in the hall.
He saw the man at the grand get up.

In the street was blackout because of the strike.
Droshkies wheeled by swiftly in the night.

AFTER THE ATTACK

The sick boy.
Locked in a vision
with tongue stiff as a horn.

He sits with his back towards the painting of a wheatfield.
The bandage around his jaw reminds one of an embalming.
His spectacles are thick as a diver's. Nothing has any answer
and is sudden as a telephone ringing in the night.

But the painting there. It is a landscape that makes one feel peaceful even
    though the wheat is a golden storm.
Blue, fiery blue sky and driving clouds. Beneath in the yellow waves
some white shirts are sailing: threshers—they cast no shadow.

At the far end of the field a man seems to be looking this way. A broad hat
    leaves his face in shadow.
He seems to look at the dark shape in the room here, as though to help.
Gradually the painting begins to stretch and open behind the boy who is
    sick
and sunk in himself. It throws sparks and makes noise. Every wheathead
    throws off light as if to wake him up!
The other man—in the wheat—makes a sign.

He has come nearer.
No one notices it.

THE JOURNEY'S
FORMULAE

(from the Balkans, 1955)

I

A murmur of voices behind the plowman.
He doesn't look round. The empty fields.
A murmur of voices behind the plowman.
One by one the shadows break loose
and plunge into the summer sky's abyss.

II

Four oxen come, under the sky.
Nothing proud about them. And the dust thick
as wool. The insects' pens scrape.

A swirl of horses, lean as in
gray allegories of the plague.
Nothing gentle about them. And the sun raves.

III

The stable smell of the village with thin dogs.
The party official in the market square
in the stable smell of the village with white houses.

His heaven accompanies him: it is high
and narrow like inside a minaret.
The wing-trailing village on the hillside.

IV

An old house has shot itself in the forehead.
Two boys kick a ball in the twilight.
A swarm of rapid echoes.—Suddenly, starlight.

V

On the road in the long darkness. My wristwatch
gleams obstinately with time's imprisoned insect.

The quiet in the crowded compartment is dense.
In the darkness the meadows stream past.

But the writer is halfway into his image, there
he travels, at the same time eagle and mole.

3

FROM
*THE HALF-FINISHED
HEAVEN*
(1962)

THE COUPLE

They turn the light off, and its white globe glows
an instant and then dissolves, like a tablet
in a glass of darkness. Then a rising.
The hotel walls shoot up into heaven's darkness.

Their movements have grown softer, and they sleep,
but their most secret thoughts begin to meet
like two colors that meet and run together
on the wet paper in a schoolboy's painting.

It is dark and silent. The city however has come nearer
tonight. With its windows turned off. Houses have come.
They stand packed and waiting very near,
a mob of people with blank faces.

FACE TO FACE

In February living stood still.
The birds flew unwillingly and the soul
chafed against the landscape as a boat
chafes against the pier it lies moored to.

The trees stood with their backs turned towards me.
The deep snow was measured with dead straws.
The footprints grew old out on the crust.
Under a tarpaulin language pined.

One day something came to the window.
Work was dropped, I looked up.
The colors flared. Everything turned round.
The earth and I sprang towards each other.

THROUGH THE
FOREST

A spot they call Jacob's marsh
is the cellar of the summer day
where light sours to a drink
tasting of old age and slums.

Here the weak giants stand entangled
so thickly they cannot fall.
A broken birch tree molders
standing upright like a dogma.

From the deeps of the forest I rise.
It lightens between the trunks of trees.
It rains over my roofs.
I'm impression's water spout.

At the edge of the forest the air is mild.—
A big fir, dark, back turned,
its muzzle buried in the soil,
is drinking the shadow of the rain.

NOVEMBER LUSTER
OF PRECIOUS FURS

Precisely because the sky is gray
the ground itself becomes luminous:
the fields with their shy green,
and the blood-bread-colored soil.

There is the red wall of a barn.
And there are meadows under water
like shining rice fields in some Asia—
where sea gulls land and reminisce.

Haze-filled spaces in the forest
gently ringing as they touch,
an inspiration that lives hidden
and flees into the forest like Nils Dacke.*

*Nils Dacke, d. 1543, leader in a peasants' war.
Although initially victorious, Dacke's peasant
army was defeated. He was declared an outlaw,
and had to flee into the forests of Blekinge in
southern Sweden.

JOURNEY

On the subway platform.
A crowd among billboards
in a staring dead light.

The train comes and fetches
faces and briefcases.

Darkness next. We sit
like statues in the cars
hauled into the tunnels.
Strain, dreams, strain.

At stations below sea level
the news of darkness is sold.
People moving melancholy,
mum, beneath clockfaces.

The train carries a load
of street clothes and souls.

Looks in all directions,
passing through the mountain.
Nothing changing yet.

But near the surface begins
the hum of freedom's bees.
We emerge from the earth.

The countryside flaps its wings
once, and then subsides
under us, wide and greenish.

Shucks of corn blow in
across the platforms.

End of the line! I ride
beyond the end of the line.

How many aboard? Four,
five, hardly more.

Houses, roads, skies,
fjords, mountains
have opened their windows.

C MAJOR

When he came down to the street after the rendezvous
the air was swirling with snow.
Winter had come
while they lay together.
The night shone white.
He walked quickly with joy.
The whole town was downhill.
The smiles passing by—
everyone was smiling behind turned-up collars.
It was free!
And all the question marks began singing of God's being.
So he thought.

A music broke out
and walked in the swirling snow
with long steps.
Everything on the way towards the note C.
A trembling compass directed at C.
One hour higher than the torments.
It was easy!
Behind turned-up collars everyone was smiling.

FROM THE MOUNTAIN

I stand on the mountain and look across the bay.
The boats rest on the surface of summer.
"We are sleepwalkers. Moons adrift."
So say the white sails.

"We slip through a sleeping house.
We gently open the doors.
We lean towards freedom."
So say the white sails.

Once I saw the wills of the world sailing.
They held the same course—one single fleet.
"We are dispersed now. No one's escort."
So say the white sails.

ESPRESSO

Black coffee at sidewalk cafés
with chairs and tables like gaudy insects.

It is a precious sip we intercept
filled with the same strength as Yes and No.

It is fetched out of gloomy kitchens
and looks into the sun without blinking.

In daylight a dot of wholesome black
quickly drained by the wan patron . . .

Like those black drops of profundity
sometimes absorbed by the soul

that give us a healthy push: Go!
The courage to open our eyes.

THE PALACE

We went in. An enormous hall,
hushed, vacant, the floor bare,
like ice in an abandoned rink.
The doors closed. The air, gray.

Paintings on the walls. We saw
swarming still lifes: shields, scale-
pans, fish, struggling forms
competing in a deaf-mute mirror world.

A sculpture was installed in the void:
alone and central stood a horse,
but at first we did not notice it,
having been captured by the void.

Softer than the whisper in a shell
noises and voices from the town
we heard circling in the empty room,
muttering in their search for power.

Also something else. Something dark
stationed itself at the threshold
of our five senses but couldn't pass.
Silent sand ran in the hourglass.

Time we bestirred ourselves. We moved
towards the horse. It was gigantic,
black as iron. The image of power itself,
still here, though sovereigns have vanished.

The horse spoke: "I am the Only One.
The vacancy that rode me I have thrown.
This is my stable. I am growing slowly.
And I eat the silence here."

IN THE NILE DELTA

The young wife cried right in her food
in the hotel after a day in the town
where she had seen the sick who crawled and lay about
and children who had to die from want.

She and her husband went up to their room
where water was sprinkled to hold down the dust.
Each went to bed with few words.
She fell into a heavy sleep. He lay awake.

Out in the dark a loud clamor streamed by.
Murmurs, tramping, shouts, wagons, song.
It went on in poverty. It never ended.
And he fell asleep curled up in a "no."

A dream came. He was on a sea voyage.
In the gray water there rose up a disturbance
and a voice said: "There is one who is good.
There is one who can see without hating."

A SWIMMING
DARK FIGURE

A prehistoric painting
on a cliff in the Sahara:
a swimming dark figure
in an old river that's young.

Without weapons or strategy,
neither resting nor running
and cut off from his own shadow:
it glides on the river's bottom.

He fought to get himself free
from a slumbering green picture,
to at last come forth to the shore
and be one with his own shadow.

LAMENTO

He put the pen down.
It lies there without moving.
It lies there without moving in empty space.
He put the pen down.

So much that can neither be written nor kept inside!
His body is stiffened by something happening far away
though the curious overnight bag beats like a heart.

Outside, the late spring.
From the foliage a whistling—people or birds?
And the cherry trees in bloom pat the heavy trucks on the way home.

Weeks go by.
Slowly night comes.
Moths settle down on the pane:
small pale telegrams from the world.

ALLEGRO

After a black day, I play Haydn,
and feel a little warmth in my hands.

The keys are ready. Kind hammers fall.
The sound is spirited, green, and full of silence.

The sound says that freedom exists
and someone pays no tax to Caesar.

I shove my hands in my haydnpockets
and act like a man who is calm about it all.

I raise my haydnflag. The signal is:
"We do not surrender. But want peace."

The music is a house of glass standing on a slope;
rocks are flying, rocks are rolling.

The rocks roll straight through the house
but every pane of glass is still whole.

THE HALF-FINISHED
HEAVEN

Despondency breaks off its course.
Anguish breaks off its course.
The vulture breaks off its flight.

The eager light streams out,
even the ghosts take a drink.

And our paintings see daylight,
our red beasts of the ice-age studios.

Everything begins to look around.
We walk in the sun in hundreds.

Each man is a half-open door
leading to a room for everyone.

The endless ground under us.

The water is shining among the trees.

The lake is a window into the earth.

NOCTURNE

I drive through a village at night, the houses step out
into the headlights—they are awake now, they want a drink.
Houses, barns, nameposts, deserted trailers—now
they take on life. Human beings sleep:

some can sleep peacefully, others have tense faces
as though in hard training for eternity.
They don't dare to let go even in deep sleep.
They wait like lowered gates while the mystery rolls past.

Outside town the road sweeps on a long time through the forest.
Trees, trees silent in a pact with each other.
They have a melodramatic color, as if in firelight.
How clear every leaf is! They follow me all the way home.

I lie about to fall asleep, I see unknown images
and signs sketching themselves behind the eyelids
on the wall of the dark. In the slot between waking and sleep
a large letter tries to get in without quite succeeding.

A WINTER NIGHT

The storm puts its mouth to the house
    and blows to produce a note.
I sleep uneasily, turn, with shut eyes
    read the storm's text.

But the child's eyes are large in the dark
    and for the child the storm howls.
Both are fond of lamps that swing.
    Both are halfway towards speech.

The storm has childish hands and wings.
    The Caravan bolts towards Lapland.
And the house feels its own constellation of nails
    holding the walls together.

The night is calm over our floor
    (where all expired footsteps
rest like sunk leaves in a pond)
    but outside the night is wild.

Over the world goes a graver storm.
    It sets its mouth to our soul
And blows to produce a note. We dread
    that the storm will blow us empty.

4

FROM
BELLS AND TRACKS
(1966)

FROM AN AFRICAN DIARY (1963)

In the painting of the kitsch Congolese artists
The figures are skinny as insects, their human energy saddened.
The road from one way of life to another is hard.
The one who has arrived has a long way to go.

A young African found a tourist lost among the huts.
He couldn't decide whether to make him a friend or object of blackmail.
The indecision upset him. They parted in confusion.

Europeans stick near their cars as if the cars were Mama.
Cicadas are strong as electric razors. The cars drive home.
Soon the lovely darkness comes and washes the dirty clothes. Sleep.
The one who has arrived has a long way to go.

Perhaps a migratory flock of handshakes would help.
Perhaps letting the truth escape from books would help.
We have to go farther.

The student studies all night, studies and studies so he can be free.
When the examination is over, he turns into a stair-rung for the next man.
A hard road.
The one who has arrived has a long way to go.

CRESTS

With a sigh the elevators start rising
in high blocks delicate as porcelain.
It will be a hot day out on the asphalt.
The traffic signs have drooping eyelids.

The land a steep slope to the sky.
Crest after crest, no proper shadow.
We fly there on the hunt for You
through the summer in Cinemascope.

And in the evening I lie like a ship
with lights out, just at the right distanc
from reality, while the crew
swarm in the parks there ashore.

HOMMAGES

Walked along the antipoetic wall.
Die Mauer. Don't look over.
It wants to surround our adult lives
in the routine city, the routine landscape.

Eluard touched some button
and the wall opened
and the garden showed itself.

I used to go with the milk pail through the wood.
Purple trunks on all sides.
An old joke hung in there
as beautiful as a votive ship.

Summer read out of *Pickwick Papers*.
The good life, a tranquil carriage
crowded with excited gentlemen.

Close your eyes, change horses.

In distress come childish thoughts.
We sat by the sickbed and prayed
for a pause in the terror, a breach
where the Pickwicks could pull in.

Close your eyes, change horses.

It is easy to love fragments
that have been on the way a long time.
Inscriptions on church bells
and proverbs written across saints
and many-thousand-year-old seeds.

Archilochos!—No answer.

The birds roamed over the seas' rough pelt.
We locked ourselves in with Simenon
and felt the smell of human life
where the serials debouch.

Feel the smell of truth.

The open window has stopped
in front of the treetops here
and the evening sky's farewell letter.

Shiki, Björling and Ungaretti
with life's chalks on death's blackboard.
The poem which is completely possible.

I looked up when the branches swung.
White gulls were eating black cherries.

WINTER'S FORMULAE

I
I went to sleep in my bed
and awoke under the keel.

In the morning, four o'clock,
when bones, scoured clean,
collect together coldly.

I went to sleep among swallows
and awoke among eagles.

II
In lamplight, ice on the road
glistens like lard.

This is not Africa.
This is not Europe.
This is nowhere but "here."

And what was "I"
is only a word
in December's dark mouth.

III
The hospital pavilions
glow against the darkness
like lighted TV screens.

A hidden tuning fork
in the immense cold
emits its ringing hum.

I stand under starry sky
and feel the world crawl

in and out of my coat
as in an anthill.

IV
Three black oaks jut out of snow.
So rough, but nimble-fingered.
From their ample bottles
greenery will foam this spring.

V
The bus crawls through winter dusk
like a ship aglow among pines
where the road is a narrow, deep, dead canal.

Few passengers: some old, some youngsters.
If the bus stopped, with its lights out,
the whole world would be obliterated.

MORNING BIRDS

I wake my car.
Its windshield is covered with pollen.
I put on my sunglasses
and the song of the birds darkens.

While another man buys a newspaper
in the railroad station
near a large freight car
which is entirely red with rust
and stands flickering in the sun.

No emptiness anywhere here.

Straight across the spring warmth a cold corridor
where someone comes hurrying
to say that they are slandering him
all the way up to the Director.

Through a back door in the landscape
comes the magpie
black and white, Hel's bird.
And the blackbird moving crisscross
until everything becomes a charcoal drawing,
except for the white sheets on the clothesline:
a Palestrina choir.

No emptiness anywhere here.

Fantastic to feel how my poem grows
while I myself shrink.
It is growing, it takes my place.
It pushes me out of its way.
It throws me out of the nest.

ABOUT HISTORY

I

One day in March I go down to the sea and listen.
The ice is as blue as the sky. It is breaking up under the sun.
The sun which also whispers in a microphone under
                                    the covering of ice.
It gurgles and froths. And someone seems to be
                                    shaking a sheet far out.
It's all like History: our Now. We are submerged, we listen.

II

Conferences like flying islands about to crash . . .
Then: a long trembling bridge of compromises.
There shall the whole traffic go, under the stars.
under the unborn pale faces,
outcast in the vacant spaces, anonymous as grains of rice.

III

Goethe traveled in Africa in '26 disguised as Gide
                                    and saw everything.
Some faces become clearer from everything
                                    they see after death.
When the daily news from Algeria was read out
there appeared a large house where all the windows
                                    were blacked,
all except one. And there we saw the face of Dreyfus.

IV

Radical and Reactionary live together as in an
                                    unhappy marriage,
molded by one another, dependent on one another.
But we who are their children must break loose.
Every problem cries in its own language.
Go like a bloodhound where the truth has trampled.

V

Out on the open ground not far from the buildings
an abandoned newspaper has lain for months, full of events.
It grows old through nights and days in rain and sun,
on the way to becoming a plant, a cabbage-head,
     on the way to being united with the earth.
 Just as a memory is slowly transmuted into your own self.

LONELINESS

I
One evening in February I came near to dying here.
The car skidded sideways on the ice, out
on the wrong side of the road. The approaching cars—
their lights—closed in.

My name, my girls, my job
broke free and were left silently behind
further and further away. I was anonymous
like a boy in a playground surrounded by enemies.

The approaching traffic had huge lights.
They shone on me while I pulled at the wheel
in a transparent terror that floated like egg white.
The seconds grew—there was space in them—
they grew big as hospital buildings.

You could almost pause
and breathe out for a while
before being crushed.

Then something caught: a helping grain of sand
or a wonderful gust of wind. The car broke free
and scuttled smartly right over the road.
A post shot up and cracked—a sharp clang—it
flew away in the darkness.

Then—stillness. I sat back in my seat-belt
and saw someone coming through the whirling snow
to see what had become of me.

II
I have been walking for a long time
on the frozen Östergötland fields.
I have not seen a single person.

In other parts of the world
there are people who are born, live and die
in a perpetual crowd.

To be always visible—to live
in a swarm of eyes—
a special expression must develop.
Face coated with clay.

The murmuring rises and falls
while they divide up among themselves
the sky, the shadows, the sand grains.

I must be alone
ten minutes in the morning
and ten minutes in the evening.
—Without a program.

Everyone is queuing at everyone's door.

Many.

One.

ON THE OUTSKIRTS OF WORK

In the middle of work
we start longing fiercely for wild greenery,
for the Wilderness itself, penetrated only
by the thin civilization of the telephone wires.

.

The moon of leisure circles the planet Work
with its mass and weight.—That's how they want it.
When we are on the way home the ground pricks up its ears.
The underground listens to us via the grass-blades.

.

Even in this working day there is a private calm.
As in a smoky inland area where a canal flows:
THE BOAT appears unexpectedly in the traffic
or glides out behind the factory, a white vagabond.

.

One Sunday I walk past an unpainted new building
standing before the gray water.
It is half-finished. The wood has the same light color
as the skin on someone bathing.

.

Outside the lamps the September night is totally dark.
When the eyes adjust, there is faint light
over the ground where large snails glide out
and the mushrooms are as numerous as the stars.

AFTER A DEATH

Once there was a shock
that left behind a long, shimmering comet tail.
It keeps us inside. It makes the TV pictures snowy.
It settles in cold drops on the telephone wires.

One can still go slowly on skis in the winter sun
through brush where a few leaves hang on.
They resemble pages torn from old telephone directories.
Names swallowed by the cold.

It is still beautiful to feel the heart beat
but often the shadow seems more real than the body.
The samurai looks insignificant
beside his armor of black dragon scales.

OKLAHOMA

I

The train stalled far to the south. Snow in New York,
but here we could go in shirtsleeves all night.
Yet no one was out. Only the cars
sped by in flashes of light like flying saucers.

II

> "We battlegrounds are proud
> of our many dead . . ."
> said a voice as I awakened.
>
> The man behind the counter said:
> "I'm not trying to sell anything,
> I'm not trying to sell anything,
> I just want to show you something."
> And he displayed the Indian axes.
>
> The boy said:
> "I know I have a prejudice,
> I don't want to have it, sir.
> What do you think of us?"

III

This motel is a foreign shell. With a rented car
(like a big white servant outside the door).
Nearly devoid of memory, and without profession,
I let myself sink to my midpoint.

SUMMER MEADOW

There's so much we must be witness to.
Reality wears us so thin
but here is summer at last:

a large airport—the controller brings
down planeload after planeload of frozen
people from outer space.

The grass and the flowers—here's where we land.
The grass has a green supervisor
I report to him.

DOWNPOUR OVER THE INTERIOR

The rain is hammering on the car roofs.
The thunder rumbles. The traffic slows down.
The lights are switched on in the middle of
                              the summer day.

The smoke pours down the chimneys.
All living things huddle, shut their eyes.
A movement inwards, feel life stronger.

The car is almost blind. He stops,
lights a private fire and smokes
while the water swills along the windows.

Here on a forest road, winding and out of the way
near a lake with water lilies
and a long mountain that vanishes in the rain.

Up there lie the piles of stones
from the Iron Age when this was a place
for tribal wars, a colder Congo

and the danger drove beasts and men together
to a murmuring refuge behind the walls,
behind thickets and stones on the hilltop.

A dark slope, someone moving
up clumsily with his shield on his back
—this he imagines while the car is standing.

It begins to lighten, he winds down the window.
A bird flutes away to itself
in a thinning silent rain.

The lake surface is taut. The thunder-sky whispers
down through the water lilies to the mud.
The forest windows are slowly opening.

But the thunder strikes straight out of the stillness!
A deafening clap. And then a void
where the last drops fall.

In the silence he hears an answer coming.
From far away. A kind of coarse child's voice.
It rises, a bellowing from the hill.

A roar of mingled notes.
A long-hoarse trumpet from the Iron Age.
Perhaps from inside himself.

UNDER PRESSURE

The blue sky's engine-drone is deafening.
We're living on a shuddering work-site
where the ocean depths can suddenly open up—
shells and telephones hiss.

You can see beauty only from the side, hastily.
The dense grain on the field, many colors in a yellow stream.
The restless shadows in my head are drawn there.
They want to creep into the grain and turn to gold.

Darkness falls. At midnight I go to bed.
The smaller boat puts out from the larger boat.
You are alone on the water.
Society's dark hull drifts further and further away.

OPEN AND CLOSED SPACES

A man feels the world with his work like a glove.
He rests for a while at midday having laid aside
                                the gloves on the shelf.
There they suddenly grow, spread
and black out the whole house from inside.

The blacked-out house is away out among the winds of spring.
"Amnesty," runs the whisper in the grass: "amnesty."
A boy sprints with an invisible line slanting up in the sky
where his wild dream of the future flies like a kite
                                bigger than the suburb.

Further north you can see from a summit the blue endless
                                carpet of pine forest
where the cloud shadows
are standing still.
No, are flying.

AN ARTIST IN THE NORTH

I, Edvard Grieg, moved free among men.
I joked a lot, read the papers, often on tour.
I conducted the orchestra.
The auditorium and its lights shuddered with each triumph
                like a train ferry pushing in to dock.

I have holed myself up here to butt heads with silence.
My work hut is small.
The grand piano fits as rubbing-tight in here as a swallow
                under a roof shingle.

The steep and lovely mountain slopes are silent most of the time.
There is no path
but there is a wicket that sometimes opens,
and a peculiar light leaks in directly from the trolls.

Simplify!

And hammer blows in the mountain came
came
came
came one spring night into our room
disguised as heartbeats.

The year before I die I shall send out four hymns
                to track down God.
But it begins here.
A song about that which is near.

That which is near.

Battlegrounds within us
where we Bones of the Dead
fight to come alive.

OUT IN THE OPEN

I
Late autumn labyrinth.
At the entry to the woods a thrown-away bottle.
Go in. Woods are silent abandoned houses this time of year.
Just a few sounds now: as if someone were moving twigs around carefully
    with pincers
or as if an iron hinge were whining feebly inside a thick trunk.
Frost has breathed on the mushrooms and they have shriveled up.
They look like objects and clothing left behind by people who've
    disappeared.
It will be dark soon. The thing to do now is to get out
and find the landmarks again: the rusty machine out in the field
and the house on the other side of the lake, a reddish square intense as a
    bouillon cube.

II
A letter from America drove me out again, started me walking
through the luminous June night in the empty suburban streets
among newborn districts without memories, cool as blueprints.

Letter in my pocket. Half-mad, lost walking, it is a kind of prayer.
Over there evil and good actually have faces.
For the most part with us it's a fight between roots, numbers, shades of
    light.

The people who run death's errands for him don't shy from daylight.
They rule from glass offices. They mill about in the bright sun.
They lean forward over a desk, and throw a look to the side.

Far off I found myself standing in front of one of the new buildings.
Many windows flowed together there into a single window.
In it the luminous nightsky was caught, and the walking trees.
It was a mirrorlike lake with no waves, turned on edge in the summer
    night.

Violence seemed unreal
for a few moments.

III
Sun burning. The plane comes in low
throwing a shadow shaped like a giant cross that rushes over the ground.
A man is sitting in the field poking at something.
The shadow arrives.
For a fraction of a second he is right in the center of the cross.

I have seen the cross hanging in the cool church vaults.
At times it resembles a split-second snapshot of something
moving at tremendous speed.

SLOW MUSIC

The building is closed. The sun crowds in through
                              the windowpanes
and warms up the surfaces of desks
that are strong enough to take the load of human fate.

We are outside today, on the long wide slope.
Many have dark clothes. You can stand in the sun with
                              your eyes shut
and feel yourself blown slowly forward.

I come too seldom down to the water. But I am here now,
among large stones with peaceful backs.
Stones which slowly migrated backwards up
                              out of the waves.

5

SEEING IN THE DARK
(1970)

THE NAME

I got sleepy while driving and pulled in under a tree at the side of the road. Rolled up in the back seat and went to sleep. How long? Hours. Darkness had come.

All of a sudden I was awake, and didn't know who I was. I'm fully conscious, but that doesn't help. Where am I? WHO am I? I am something that has just woken up in a back seat, throwing itself around in panic like a cat in a gunnysack. Who am I?

After a long while my life comes back to me. My name comes to me like an angel. Outside the castle walls there is a trumpet blast (as in the Leonora Overture) and the footsteps that will save me come quickly quickly down the long staircase. It's me coming! It's me!

But it is impossible to forget the fifteen-second battle in the hell of nothingness, a few feet from a major highway where the cars slip past with their lights on.

A FEW MINUTES

The squat pine in the swamp holds up its crown: a dark rag.
But what you see is nothing
compared to the roots, the widespread, secretly creeping, immortal or
    half-mortal
root system.

I you she he also branch out.
Outside what one wills.
Outside the Metropolis.

A shower falls out of the milk-white summer sky.
It feels as if my five senses were linked to another creature
which moves stubbornly
as the brightly clad runners in a stadium where the darkness streams down.

BREATHING SPACE JULY

The man who lies on his back under huge trees
is also up in them. He branches out into thousands of tiny branches.
He sways back and forth,
he sits in a catapult chair that hurtles forward in slow motion.

The man who stands down at the dock screws up his eyes against the water.
Docks get old faster than men.
They have silver-gray posts and boulders in their gut.
The dazzling light drives straight in.

The man who spends the whole day in an open boat
moving over the luminous bays
will fall asleep at last inside the shade of his blue lamp
as the islands crawl like huge moths over the globe.

BY THE RIVER

Talking with contemporaries I saw heard behind their faces
the stream
that flowed and flowed and pulled with it the willing and the unwilling.

And the creature with stuck-together eyes that wants
to go right down the rapids with the current
throws itself forward without trembling
in a furious hunger for simplicity.

The water pulls more and more heavily

as where the river narrows and goes over
in the rapids—the place where I paused
after a journey through dry woods

one June evening: the radio gives the latest
on the special meeting: Kosygin, Eban.
A few thoughts drill despairingly.
A few people down in the village.

And under the suspension bridge the masses of water hurl
past. Here comes the timber. Some logs
shoot right out like torpedoes. Others turn
crosswise, twirl sluggishly and helplessly away

and some nose against the river banks,
push among stones and rubbish, wedge fast
and pile up there like clasped hands

motionless in the uproar . . .

I saw heard from the bridge
in a cloud of mosquitoes,
together with some boys. Their bicycles
buried in the greenery—only the horns
stuck up.

OUTSKIRTS

Men in overalls the same color as earth rise from a ditch.
It's a transitional place, in stalemate, neither country nor city.
Construction cranes on the horizon want to take the big leap, but the clocks
    are against it.
Concrete piping scattered around laps at the light with cold tongues.
Auto-body shops occupy old barns.
Stones throw shadows as sharp as objects on the moon surface.
And these sites keep on getting bigger
like the land bought with Judas' silver: "a potter's field for burying strangers."

TRAFFIC

The long-distance truck with its trailer pushes through fog,
the huge silhouette of a dragonfly's larva
slowly stirring the silt on the lake's bottom.

Our headlights meet in the dripping gloom.
We can't make out each other's faces.
Floods of light plunge through pine needles.

We come, we shadowy vans from all directions,
in twilight, in tandem, shuttling single file,
gliding forward in a muffled, turned-down roar

out on the flats where industries brood,
and the building developments sink two millimeters
a year—the ground slowly swallows them.

Unidentified paws put their prints
on the shiniest product dreamed up around here.
Seeds struggle to live in the asphalt.

But first the chestnut trees go murky, as if
preparing a blossoming of iron gloves
instead of white catkins, while behind them

in the company's front office a faulty neon tube
keeps blinking blinking. There's a secret door here. Open!
and put your eye to the reversed periscope,

look down, into the gullets, into the lowest drains
where algae thrive like dead men's beards,
where The Cleaner swims in his coverall of slime

with ever feebler strokes, about to suffocate.
And no one knows how it will turn out, only that the chain
breaks and is mended again, over and over.

NIGHT DUTY

I
Tonight I am down among the ballast.
I am one of the silent weights
which prevent the ship overturning!
Obscure faces in the darkness like stones.
They can only hiss: "don't touch me."

II
Other voices throng, the listener
glides like a lean shadow over the radio's
luminous band of stations.
The language marches in step with the executioners.
Therefore we must get a new language.

III
The wolf is here, friend for every hour
touching the windows with his tongue.
The valley is full of crawling axe-handles.
The night-flyer's din pours over the sky
sluggishly, like a wheelchair with iron rims.

IV
They are digging up the town. But it is silent now.
Under the elms in the churchyard:
an empty excavator. The bucket against the earth—
the gesture of a man who has fallen asleep at table
with his fist in front of him.—Bell-ringing.

THE OPEN WINDOW

I shaved one morning standing
by the open window
on the second story.
Switched on the razor.
It started to hum.
A heavier and heavier whirr.
Grew to a roar.
Grew to a helicopter.
And a voice—the pilot's—pierced
the noise, shouting:
"Keep your eyes open!
You're seeing this for the last time!"
Rose.
Floated low over the summer.
The small things I love, have they any weight?
So many dialects of green.
And especially the red of housewalls.
Beetles glittered in the dung, in the sun.
Cellars pulled up by the roots
sailed through the air.
Industry.
Printing presses crawled along.
People at that instant
were the only things motionless.
They observe their moment of silence.
And the dead in the churchyard especially
held still
like those who posed in the infancy of the camera.
Fly low!
I didn't know which way
to turn my head—
my sight was divided
like a horse's.

PRELUDES

I

I flinch from something that shuffles slantwise through sleet.
A fragment of what is to come.
A wall broken loose. Something without eyes. Hard.
A face of teeth!
A lone wall. Or is the house there
although I do not see it?
The Future: an army of empty houses
that grope their way ahead through sleet.

II

Two truths approach each other. One comes from within,
one comes from without—and where they meet you have the chance
to catch a look at yourself.
Noticing what is about to happen, you shout desperately: "Stop!
Anything, anything, as long as I don't have to know myself."

And there is a boat that wants to put in—tries to, right here—
it will try again thousands of times.
Out of the forest's dark comes a long boat hook
that's pushed through the open window
among the party guests who have danced themselves warm.

III

The apartment I've lived in most of my life is to be evacuated. It's already
emptied of everything. The anchor has let go—but despite the mournful
air it's still the lightest apartment in the city. Truth needs no furniture.
I've gone one round on life's circle and come back to the starting point: a
bare room. Scenes from my early life take shape on the walls like Egyptian
paintings inside a burial chamber. But they are fading. The light is too
strong. The windows have enlarged. The empty apartment is a big tele-
scope pointed at the sky. It's as quiet here as a Quaker meeting. Nothing
heard but the pigeons of the backyards, their cooings.

STANDING UP

In a split second of hard thought, I managed to catch her. I stopped, holding the hen in my hands. Strange, she didn't really feel living: rigid, dry, an old white plume-ridden lady's hat that shrieked out the truths of 1912. Thunder in the air. An odor rose from the fence-boards, as when you open a photo album that has got so old that no one can identify the people any longer.

I carried her back inside the chicken netting and let her go. All of a sudden she came back to life, she knew who she was, and ran off according to the rules. Hen-yards are thick with taboos. But the earth all around is full of affection and tenacity. A low stone wall half overgrown with leaves. When dusk begins to fall the stones are faintly luminous with the hundred-year-old warmth from the hands that built it.

It's been a hard winter, but summer is here and the fields want us to walk upright. Every man unimpeded, but careful, as when you stand up in a small boat. I remember a day in Africa: on the banks of the Chari, there were many boats, an atmosphere positively friendly, the men almost blue-black in color with three parallel scars on each cheek (meaning the Sara tribe). I am welcomed on a boat—it's a canoe hollowed from a dark tree. The canoe is incredibly wobbly, even when you sit on your heels. A balancing act. If you have the heart on the left side you have to lean a bit to the right, nothing in the pockets, no big arm movements, please, all rhetoric has to be left behind. Precisely: rhetoric is impossible here. The canoe glides out over the water.

THE BOOKCASE

It was brought from the dead woman's apartment. It stood empty a few days, empty until I filled it with books, all the bound ones, those bulky tomes. With that act I had let in the underworld. Something swelled up from below, mounted slowly, inexorably, like mercury in a gigantic thermometer. You were not allowed to turn your head away.

The black volumes, their closed faces. They're like the Algerians who stood at the Friedrichstrasse border crossing, waiting for the *Volkspolizei* to check their passports. My own passport lay a long time in various glass cubicles. And the fog all over Berlin that day, it is also in this book-case. An old despair lives in there, it tastes of Passchendaele and the Treaty of Versailles—the taste, in fact, is older than that. The black heavy tomes—I come back to them—they are themselves a sort of passport, and they are so fat because they have accumulated so many stamps through the centuries. There is one trip, apparently, for which your baggage can't be heavy enough, once you've embarked, when finally you . . .

All the old historians are there, and are invited to climb up and look into our family. Nothing can be heard, but the lips move all the time behind the glass ("Passchendaele" . . .). One is reminded of a venerable government office—now follows a true ghost story—a grand building where portraits of long-dead men hang behind glass, and one morning there appeared a blur on the inside of the glass. They had begun breathing during the night.

The bookcase is even more powerful. Glares straight across the border zone! A shimmering membrane, the shimmering membrane of a dark river in which the room is forced to mirror itself. And you must not turn your head away.

6

PATHS
(1973)

TO FRIENDS BEHIND A FRONTIER

I
I wrote so meagerly to you. But what I couldn't write
swelled and swelled like an old-fashioned airship
and drifted away at last through the night sky.

II
The letter is now at the censor's. He lights his lamp.
In the glare my words fly up like monkeys on a grille,
rattle it, stop, and bare their teeth.

III
Read between the lines. We'll meet in 200 years
when the microphones in the hotel walls are forgotten
and can at last sleep, become trilobites.

FROM THE THAW OF
1966

Headlong headlong waters; roaring; old hypnosis.
The river swamps the car-cemetery, glitters
behind the masks.
I hold tight to the bridge railing.
The bridge: a big iron bird sailing past death.

SKETCH IN OCTOBER

The towboat is freckled with rust. What's it doing here so far inland?
It is a heavy extinguished lamp in the cold.
But the trees have wild colors: signals to the other shore.
As if people wanted to be fetched.

On my way home I see mushrooms sprouting
                              up through the lawn.
They are the fingers, stretching for help, of someone
who has long sobbed to himself in the darkness down there.
We are the earth's.

FURTHER IN

It's the main highway leading in,
the sun soon down.
Traffic backs up, creeps along,
it's a torpid glittering dragon.
I am a scale on that dragon.
The red sun all at once
blazes in my windshield,
pouring in,
and makes me transparent.
Some writing shows
up inside me—words
written with invisible ink
appearing when the paper
is held over a fire.
I know that I have to go far away,
straight through the city, out
the other side, then step out
and walk a long time in the woods.
Walk in the tracks of the badger.
Growing hard to see, nearly dark.
Stones lie about on the moss.
One of those stones is precious.
It can change everything.
It can make the darkness shine.
It's the light switch for the whole country.
Everything depends on it.
Look at it . . . touch it . . .

GUARD DUTY

I'm ordered out to a big hump of stones
as if I were an aristocratic corpse from the Iron Age.
The rest are still back in the tent sleeping,
stretched out like spokes in a wheel.

In the tent the stove is boss: it is a big snake
that swallows a ball of fire and hisses.
But it is silent out here in the spring night
among chill stones waiting for the dawn.

Out here in the cold I start to fly
like a shaman, straight to her body—
some places pale from her swimming suit.
The sun shone right on us. The moss was hot.

I brush along the side of warm moments,
but I can't stay there long.
I'm whistled back through space—
I crawl among the stones. Back to here and now.

Task: to be where I am.
Even when I'm in this solemn and absurd
role: I am still the place
where creation works on itself.

Dawn comes, the sparse tree trunks
take on color now, the frostbitten
forest flowers form a silent search party
after something that has disappeared in the dark.

But to be where I am . . . and to wait.
I am full of anxiety, obstinate, confused.
Things not yet happened are already here!
I feel that. They're just out there:

a murmuring mass outside the barrier.
They can only slip in one by one.
They want to slip in. Why? They do
one by one. I am the turnstile.

ALONG THE LINES

I
Sun glints from the frozen river.
This is the world's roof.
Silence.

I sit on an overturned boat, pulled up on shore,
swallow the silence-potion,
I am slowly turning.

II
A wheel stretches out endlessly, is turning.
The hub is here, is nearly
motionless.

Some motion farther out: tracks in the snow,
words that begin to slide
past building fronts.

The hum of traffic from the highway
and the traffic without sound
of the dead as they return.

Farther out: tragic masks bracing the wind,
the roar of acceleration—still farther
the rushing

where the last words of love evaporate—
water drops that creep slowly
down steel wings . . .

profiles shouting—the empty earphones
clashing against each other—
kamikaze!

III
The frozen river gleams and is silent.
Shadows here are deep
and without voice.

My steps here were explosions in the field
that are now being painted by silence
painted by silence.

SEEING THROUGH
THE GROUND

The white sun melts away in the smog.
The light drips, works its way down

to my underground eyes that are there
under the city, and they see the city

from beneath: streets, foundations of houses—
like aerial photos of a wartime city

though reversed: a mole photograph . . .
speechless rectangles in gloomy colors.

Things are decided there. No one can tell
the bones of the dead from those of the living.

The sunshine increases, floods into
cockpits and into peapods.

DECEMBER EVENING 1972

Here I come, the invisible man, perhaps employed
by a Great Memory to live right now. And I am driving past

the locked-up white church—a wooden saint is standing in there
smiling, helpless, as if they had taken away his glasses.

He is alone. Everything else is now, now, now. The
                                           law of gravity pressing us
against our work by day and against our beds by night. The war.

THE SCATTERED
CONGREGATION

I

We got ready and showed our home.
The visitor thought: you live well.
The slum must be inside you.

II

Inside the church, pillars and vaulting
white as plaster, like the cast
around the broken arm of faith.

III

Inside the church there's a begging bowl
that slowly lifts from the floor
and floats along the pews.

IV

But the church bells have gone underground.
They're hanging in the sewage pipes.
Whenever we take a step, they ring.

V

Nicodemus the sleepwalker is on his way
to the Address. Who's got the Address?
Don't know. But that's where we're going.

LATE MAY

Apple trees and cherry trees in flower help the town to float
in the soft smudgy May night, white life-vests, thoughts go far away.
Stubborn grass and weeds beat their wings.
The mailbox shines calmly: what is written cannot be taken back.

A mild cooling wind goes through your shirt, feeling for the heart.
Apple trees and cherry trees laugh soundlessly at Solomon.
They blossom in my tunnel. And I need them
not to forget, but to remember.

ELEGY

I open the first door.
It is a large sunlit room.
A heavy car passes outside
and makes the china quiver.

I open door number two.
Friends! You drank some darkness
and became visible.

Door number three. A narrow hotel room.
View on an alley.
One lamppost shines on the asphalt.
Experience, its beautiful slag.

7

BALTICS (1974)

BALTICS

I
It was before the time of radio masts.

My grandfather was a newly licensed pilot. In the almanac he wrote down
   the vessels he piloted—
name, destination, draft:
Examples from 1884:
Steamer Tiger Capt Rowan 16 feet Gefle Furusund
Brig Ocean Capt Andersen 8 feet Sandofjord Hernosand Furusund
Steamer St Petersburg Capt Libenberg 11 feet Stettin Libau Sandhamn

He took them out to the Baltic, through that wonderful labyrinth of islands
   and water.
And those that met on board, and were carried by the same hull for a few
   hours or a few days,
how well did they get to know each other?
Talking in misspelled English, understanding and misunderstanding, but
   very little conscious lying.
How well did they get to know each other?

When it was thick fog: half speed, almost blind. The headland coming out
   of the invisibility with a single stride, it was right on them.
Foghorn blasting every other minute. His eyes reading straight into the
   invisible.
(Did he have the labyrinth in his head?)
The minutes went by.
Lands and reefs memorized like hymn verses.
And the feeling of we're-right-here that you have to keep, like carrying a
   pail filled to the brim without spilling a drop.

A glance down into the engine room.
The compound engine, as long-lived as a human heart, worked with great
   soft recoiling movements, steel acrobatics, and the smells rising from it
   as from a kitchen.

II
The wind walks in the pine forest. It sighs heavily, lightly.
In the middle of the forest the Baltic also sighs, deep in the forest you're
    out on the open sea.
The old woman hated the sighing in the trees, her face hardened in melancholy
    when the wind rose:
"You have to think of those out there in the boats."
But she also heard something else in the sighing, as I do, we're related.
(We're walking together. She's been dead for thirty years.)
It sighs yes and no, understanding and misunderstanding.
It sighs three children healthy, one in the sanitarium and two dead.
The broad current that blows some flames into life and blows others out.
    Conditions.
It sighs: Save me, Lord, the waters are come unto my soul.
You walk around listening for a long time, finally reaching the point where
    the boundaries begin to open out
or rather
where everything becomes boundaries. An open square sunk in darkness.
    People streaming out of the dimly lit buildings around it. A murmuring.

A new gust of wind and the square again lies solitary and still.

A new gust of wind that sighs of other shores.
It deals with war.
It deals with places where the citizens are controlled,
where thoughts are built with emergency exits,
where a conversation between friends is really a test of what friendship
    means.
And when you're together with somebody you don't know well. Control.
    A certain frankness is all right
if you just don't lose sight of something drifting there on the outskirts of
    the conversation: something dark, a dark stain,
something that can drift in
and destroy everything. Don't lose sight of it!

What can it be compared with? A mine?
No, that would be too solid. And almost too peaceful—since on our coast
  most stories about mines end happily, the terror limited to the moment.
As this story from the lightship: "Fall 1915 we were sleeping
  uneasily . . ." etc. A drifting mine was sighted
as it floated calmly toward the lightship, it was sinking, heaving up, at
  times hidden by the waves, at times glimpsed like a spy in the crowd.
The crew lying there in agony, shooting at it with rifles. Without success.
  Finally they put out a boat
and made a long line fast to the mine and towed it carefully and slowly in
  to the experts.
Afterwards they set up the mine's dark shell in a sandy little stretch of park
  as an ornament
along with Strombus Gigas shells from the West Indies.

And the gale makes its way through the dry pines beyond, it hurries over
  the sand of the cemetery,
past the leaning stones, the names of the pilots.
The dry sighing
of large gates opening and large gates closing.

III
In the half-dark corner of Gotland church, in the mildewed daylight
stands a sandstone baptismal font—12th century—the stonecutter's name
still there, shining
like a row of teeth in a mass grave:
                    HEGWALDR
                         the name still there. And his scenes
here and on the sides of other vessels crowded with people, figures on their
  way out of the stone.
The eyes' kernel of good and evil bursting there.
Herod at the table: the roasted cock flying up and crowing "Christus natus
  est"—the servant executed—

close by the child born, under clumps of faces as worthy and helpless as
   young monkeys.
And the fleeing steps of the pious
drumming over the dragon scales of sewer mouths.
(The scenes stronger in memory than when you stand in front of them,
strongest when the font spins like a slow, rumbling carousel in the memory.)
Nowhere the lee-side. Everywhere risk.
As it was. As it is.
Only inside there is peace, in the water of the vessel that
       no one sees,
but on the outer walls the struggle rages.
And peace can come drop by drop, perhaps at night
when we don't know anything,
or as when we're taped to a drip in a hospital ward.

People, beasts, ornaments.
There isn't any landscape. Ornaments.

Mr. B———, my traveling companion, amiable, in exile,
escaped from Robben Island, says:
"I envy you. I don't feel anything for nature.
But *figures in landscape,* that says something to me."

Here are figures in landscape.
A photo from 1865. The steamer lies at the dock in the channel.
Five figures. A lady in light crinoline, like a bell, like a flower.
The men are like extras in a folk play.
They're all good-looking, indecisive, beginning to fade out.
They step onshore for a moment. They fade out.
The steamer is an extinct model—
a high funnel, awning, narrow hull—
it's completely strange, a UFO that's landed.
Everything else in the photo is shockingly real:

the ripples on the water,
the opposite beach—
I can stroke the rough rocks with my hand,
I can hear the sighing in the spruce.
It's near. It's
today.
The waves are topical.

Now, a hundred years later. The waves come in from no man's water
and break against the stones.
I walk along the beach. It isn't like it used to be to walk along the beach.
You have to swallow too much, keep too many conversations going at the
    same time, you have thin walls.
Everything's gotten a new shadow behind its ordinary shadow,
and you hear it dragging along even when it's completely dark.

It's night.

The strategic planetarium rotates. The lenses stare into the darkness.
The night sky is full of numbers, and they're fed into
a blinking cupboard,
a piece of furniture,
inside it the energy of a grasshopper swarm that devours the acres of Somalia
    in half an hour.

I don't know if we're in the beginning or in the final stage.
No conclusion can be made, no conclusion is possible.
The conclusion is the mandrake—
(see the encylopedia of superstitions:
                    MANDRAKE
                                miracle-working plant
that gave such a dreadful shriek when it was torn out of the earth
that the person fell dead. A dog had to do it . . .)

IV
From the lee-side,
close-ups.

Bladderwrack. The forests of bladderwrack shine in the clear water, they're
young, you want to emigrate there, stretch out on your
own reflection and sink down to such and such a depth—
the seaweed holding itself up with air bladders, as we
hold ourselves up with ideas.

Bullhead. The fish that's a toad that wanted to be a butterfly and
made it a third of the way, hiding himself in the seaweed,
but pulled up in the net, hooked fast by his pathetic spikes
and warts—when you untangle him from the mesh of the
net your hands shine with slime.

The rocks. The small creatures hurry over the sun-warmed lichens,
rushing like second hands—the pine casts a shadow, it
wanders slowly like an hour hand—inside me time stands
still, endless time, the time it takes to forget all languages
and invent perpetual motion.

On the lee-side you can hear the grass growing, a faint drumming coming
from underneath, a faint roar of millions of small gas flames,
so it is to hear the grass grow.

And now: the stretch of open water, without doors, the open boundaries
that grow broader and broader
the further you stretch out.

There are days when the Baltic is a calm, limitless roof.
Then dream innocently of someone crawling out on the roof to try to put
   the halyards in order,

trying to hoist
the rag—

the flag that's so frayed by the wind and smoked by the funnels and
   bleached by the sun that it could be anybody's.

But it's a long way to Liepāja.

V

July 30.   The channel has become eccentric—today it's teeming with
             jellyfish for the first time in years, they pump themselves
             along with calm consideration, they belong to the same
             shipping company: AURELIA, they drift like flowers after a
             burial at sea, if you take them out of the water all of their
             shape disappears, as when an indescribable truth is lifted
             up out of the silence and formulated into a lifeless mass,
             yes, they're untranslatable, they have to stay in their
             element.

August 2.   Something wants to be said, but the words don't agree.
Something that can't be said,
aphasia,
there aren't any words but maybe a style . . .

Sometimes you wake up at night
and quickly throw some words down
on the nearest paper, on the margin of a newspaper
(the words glowing with meaning!)
but in the morning: the same words don't say anything anymore, scrawls,
   misspeakings.
Or fragments of a great nightly style that dragged past?

Music comes to a person, he's a composer, he's played, has a career, becomes
   director of the conservatory.

The trend turns downward, he's blamed by the authorities.
They put up his pupil K——— as chief prosecutor.
He's threatened, demoted, sent away.
After some years the disgrace diminishes, he's rehabilitated.
Then comes the stroke: right-side paralysis and aphasia, can only grasp
    short phrases, says wrong words.
Can, as a result of this, not be touched by advancement or blame.

But the music's still there, he still composes in his own style,
he becomes a medical sensation for the time he has left to live.

He wrote music to texts he no longer understood—
in the same way
we express something with our lives
in that humming chorus of misspeech.

The Death lectures went on for several terms. I was present
together with classmates I didn't know
(who are you?)
—afterwards everyone went off on his own, profiles.

I looked at the sky and the earth and straight ahead
and since then I've been writing a long letter to the dead
on a typewriter that doesn't have a ribbon, only a horizon line
so the words beat in vain and nothing stays.

I stand with my hand on the door handle, take the pulse of the house.
The walls so full of life
(the children won't dare sleep alone up in the attic—what makes me feel
    safe makes them uneasy.)

August 3.   Out there in the damp grass
slithers a greeting from the Middle Ages: Helix pomatia
the subtly gray-gold shining snail with its jaunty house,

introduced by some monks who liked *escargots*—yes, the Franciscans were
    here,
broke stone and burnt lime, the island was theirs in 1288, a donation
    from King Magnus
("Thes almes and othres he hath yeven / Thei meteth hym nu he entreth
    hevene.")
the forest fell, the ovens burned, the lime taken by sail
to the building of the monastery . . .

                                       Sister snail
stands almost still in the grass, feelers sucked in
and rolled out, disturbances and hesitation . . .
How like myself in my searching!

The wind that blew so carefully all day—
all the blades of grass are counted on the furthest islets—
has laid down in the middle of the island. The matchstick's flame stands
    straight up.
The sea painting and the forest painting darken together.
Also the foliage of the five-story trees is turning black.
"Every summer is the last." These are empty words
for the creatures at late summer midnight
where the crickets sew on their machines as if possessed
and the Baltic's near
and the lonely water tap stands among the wild rose bushes
like an equestrian statue. The water tastes of iron.

VI
My grandmother's story before it's forgotten: her parents dying young,
the father first. When the widow realizes the disease will take her too,
she walks from house to house, sails from island to island
with her daughter. "Who can take care of Maria?"
A strange house on the other side of the bay takes her in.
They could afford to do it. But the ones that could afford it weren't the
    good ones.

Piety's mask cracks. Maria's childhood ends too soon,
she's an unpaid servant, in perpetual coldness.
Year after year. Perpetually seasick behind the
long oars, the solemn terror
at the table, the expressions, the pike skin crunching
in her mouth: be grateful, be grateful.

                                     She never looked back.
But because of this she could see The New
and seize it.
Break out of the bonds.

I remember her, I used to snuggle against her
and at the moment she died (the moment she passed over?) she sent out
   a thought
so that I, a five-year-old, understood what had happened
half an hour before they called.

I remember her. But in the next brown photo
someone I don't know—
by the clothes from the middle of the last century.
A man about thirty, the powerful eyebrows,
the face that looks me right in the eye
whispering: "Here I am."
But who "I" am
is something no one remembers anymore. No one.

TB? Isolation?

Once he stopped
on the stony, grass-streaming slope coming up from the sea
and felt the black blindfold in front of his eyes.

Here, behind the thick brush—is it the island's oldest house?
The low, knot-trimmed two-hundred-year-old fisherman's hut, with coarse,
   gray, heavy beams.

And the modern brass padlock has clicked together on all of it, shining
   like the ring in the nose of an old bull
that refuses to get up.
So much crouching wood. And on the roof the ancient tiles that collapsed
   across and on top of each other
(the original pattern erased by the earth's rotation through the years)
it reminds me of something . . . I was there . . . wait: it's the old Jewish
   cemetery in Prague
where the dead live closer together than they did in life, the stones jammed
   in, jammed in.
So much encircled love! The tiles with the lichen's letters in an unknown
   language
are the stones in the archipelago people's ghetto cemetery, the stones
   erected and fallen down—

The ramshackle hut shines
with the light of all the people carried by the certain wave, the certain
   wind,
out here to their fates.

8

FROM
TRUTH-BARRIERS (1978)

CITOYENS

The night after the accident I dreamt of a pockmarked man
who walked along alleys singing.
Danton!
Not the other one—Robespierre took no such walks.
He spent one hour each day
on his morning toilette, the rest he gave to the People.
In the heaven of pamphleteering, among the machines of virtue.
Danton
(or the man who wore his mask)
seemed to stand on stilts.
I saw his face from underneath:
like the pitted moon, half lit, half in mourning.
I wanted to say something.
A weight in the chest: the lead weight
that makes the clocks go,
makes the hands go around: Year I, Year II . . .
A pungent odor as from sawdust in tiger cages.
And—as always in dreams—no sun.
But the alley walls
shone as they curved away
down towards the waiting-room, the curved space,
the waiting-room where we all . . .

STREET CROSSING

Cold winds hit my eyes, and two or three suns
dance in the kaleidoscope of tears, as I cross
this street I know so well,
where the Greenland summer shines from snowpools.

The street's massive life swirls around me;
it remembers nothing and desires nothing.
Far under the traffic, deep in earth,
the unborn forest waits, still, for a thousand years.

It seems to me that the street can see me.
Its eyesight is so poor the sun itself
is a gray ball of yarn in black space.
But for a second I am lit. It sees me.

THE CLEARING

Deep in the forest there's an unexpected clearing which can be reached only by someone who has lost his way.

The clearing is enclosed in a forest that is choking itself. Black trunks with the ashy beard-stubble of lichen. The trees are screwed tightly together and are dead right up to the tops, where a few solitary green twigs touch the light. Beneath them: shadow brooding on shadow, and the swamp growing.

But in the open space the grass is strangely green and living. There are big stones lying here as if they'd been arranged. They must be the foundation stones of a house, but I could be wrong. Who lived here? No one can tell us. The names exist somewhere in an archive that no one opens (it's only archives that stay young). The oral tradition has died and with it the memories. The gypsy people remember but those who have learnt to write forget. Write down, and forget.

The homestead murmurs with voices, it is the center of the world. But the inhabitants die or move out, the chronicle breaks off. Desolate for many years. And the homestead becomes a sphinx. At last everything's gone, except the foundation stones.

Somehow I've been here before, but now I must go. I dive in among the thickets. I can push my way through only with one step forward and two to the side, like a chess knight. Bit by bit the forest thins and lightens. My steps get longer. A footpath creeps towards me. I am back in the communications network.

On the humming electricity-post a beetle is sitting in the sun. Beneath the shining wing-covers its wings are folded up as ingeniously as a parachute packed by an expert.

HOW THE LATE AUTUMN NIGHT
NOVEL BEGINS

The ferryboat smells of oil and something rattles all the time like an obsession. The spotlight's turned on. We're pulling in to the jetty. I'm the only one who wants off here. "Need the gangway?" No. I take a long tottering stride right into the night and stand on the jetty, on the island. I feel wet and unwieldy, a butterfly just crept out of its cocoon, the plastic bags in each hand are misshapen wings. I turn round and see the boat gliding away with its shining windows, then grope my way towards the familiar house which has been empty for so long. There's no one in any of the houses round about. . . . It's good to fall asleep here. I lie on my back and don't know if I'm asleep or awake. Some books I've read pass by like old sailing ships on their way to the Bermuda triangle to vanish without a trace. . . . I hear a hollow sound, an absentminded drumming. An object the wind keeps knocking against something the earth holds still. If the night is not just an absence of light, if the night really *is* something, then it's that sound. Stethoscope noises from a slow heart, it beats, goes silent for a time, comes back. As if the creature were moving in a zigzag across the Frontier. Or someone knocking in a wall, someone who belongs to the other world but was left behind here, knocking, wanting back. Too late. Couldn't get down there, couldn't get up there, couldn't get aboard. . . . The other world is this world too. Next morning I see a sizzling golden-brown branch. A crawling stack of roots. Stones with faces. The forest is full of abandoned monsters which I love.

FOR MATS AND LAILA

The International Date Line lies motionless between Samoa and Tonga, but the Midnight Line slips forward over the ocean, over the islands and the hutroofs. On the other side they are asleep now. Here in Värmland it is noon, a hot day in late spring . . . I've thrown away my luggage. A dip in the sky, how blue it is . . . All at once I notice the hills on the other side of the lake: their pine has been clear-cut. They resemble the shaved skull-sections of a patient about to have a brain operation. The shaved hills have been there all the time; I never noticed them until now. Blinders and a stiff neck . . . Everything keeps moving. Now the hillsides are full of lines and dark scratches, as on those old engravings where human beings move about tiny among the foothills and mountains that resemble anthills and the villages that are thousands of lines also. And each human ant carries his own line to the big engraving; it has no real center, but is alive everywhere. One other thing: the human shapes are tiny and yet each has its own face, the engraver has allowed them that, no, they are not ants at all. Most of them are simple people but they can write their names. Proteus by comparison is a modern individual and he expresses himself fluently in all styles, comes with a message "straight from the shoulder," or one in a flowery style, depending on which gang he belongs to just now. But he can't write his own name. He draws back from that terrified, as the wolf from the silver bullet. The gangs don't want that either, the many-headed corporation doesn't want it, nor the many-headed State . . . Everything keeps moving. In the house over there a man lived who got desperate one afternoon and shot a hole in the empty hammock that was floating over the lawn. And the Midnight Line is getting close, soon it will have completed half its course. (Now don't come and ask me if I want the clock turned back!) Soon fatigue will flow in through the hole burned by the sun . . . It has never happened to me that the diamond of a certain instant cut a permanent scar on my picture of the world. No, it was the wearing, the incessant wearing away that rubbed out the light and somewhat strange smile. But something is about to become visible again, the rubbing brings it *out* this time, it is starting to resemble a smile, but no one can tell what it will be worth. Not clear yet. Somebody keeps pulling on my arm each time I try to write.

FROM THE WINTER, 1947

In the daytimes in school the dull swarming fortress.
In the evening I walked home under the signs.
Then came whispering without lips: "Wake up, sleepwalker!"
And all the objects pointed to The Room.

Fifth floor, the room over the yard. The lamp burned
in a circle of terror every night.
I sat without eyelids in the bed, seeing filmstrips
filmstrips of the thoughts of the mentally ill.

As if it were necessary . . .
As if the last of childhood were being broken into pieces
to pass through the grating.
As if it were necessary . . .

I read in a glass book, but saw only the other thing:
the stains that penetrated the wallpaper!
It was the living dead
who wanted to have their portraits painted . . .

Then at dawn came the garbage men
and clattered the garbage cans down there.
The backyard's peaceful gray bells
that rang me to sleep.

SCHUBERTIANA

I

In the evening darkness at a place outside New York, an outlook where
  you can perceive eight million people's homes in a single glance.
The giant city there is a long flickering drift, a spiral galaxy from the side.
Within the galaxy coffee cups are pushed over the counter, the shop windows
  beg from the passersby, a swarm of shoes that leave no tracks.
The clambering fire escapes, elevator doors that slip past, behind doors
  with police locks a steady swell of voices.
Slouched bodies half asleep in the subway cars, the rushing catacombs.
I know too—without statistics—that Schubert's being played in some room
  there and for someone the tones at this moment are more real than
  everything else.

II

The human brain's endless plains are crumpled up to the size of a clenched
  fist.
In April the swallow returns to her last year's nest under the gutter at just
  that barn in just that parish.
She flies from Transvaal, passes the Equator, flies for six weeks over two
  continents, steering towards that disappearing dot on the land mass.
And he who catches the signals from a whole life in some rather ordinary
  chords by a string quintet,
he who gets a river to flow through the eye of a needle
is a fat young gentleman from Vienna, called "the little mushroom" by his
  friends, who slept with his glasses on
and stood himself up punctually at his writing lectern in the morning.
At which the music script's wonderful centipedes set themselves in motion.

III

The string quintet is playing. I walk home through the humid woods with
  the ground springing under me,
huddle like one unborn, fall asleep, roll weightless into the future, know
  suddenly that the plants have thoughts.

IV

So much we have to trust to be able to live our daily day without sinking
through the earth!
Trust the masses of snow that cling to the mountainsides above the village.
Trust promises to keep silent and the understanding smile, trust that the
telegram about the accident doesn't refer to us and the sudden axe blow
from within doesn't come.
Trust the axles that carry us on the highway in the middle of the three
hundred times enlarged steel bee swarm.
But none of that is really worth our confidence.
The quintet says that we can trust something else. What else? Something
else, and it follows us a little of the way there.
Like when the light goes out on the stairs and the hand follows—with
confidence—the blind banister that finds its way in the darkness.

V

We crowd up to the piano and play with four hands in F-minor, two drivers
for the same carriage, it looks a little ridiculous.
Our hands seem to push ringing weights back and forth, as if we were
moving counterweights
in an effort to shift the large scale's frightful balance: happiness and suffering
weigh just the same.
Annie said: "This music is so heroic," and that's true.
But those who glance with furtive jealousy at men of action, those who
secretly despise themselves for not being murderers, they don't recognize
themselves here.
And the many who buy and sell people and believe that everybody can be
bought, they don't recognize themselves here,
not their music. The long melody that is itself throughout all changes,
sometimes sparkling and gentle, sometimes harsh and strong, snail track
and steel wire.
The persistent humming that follows us this very moment
up
the depths.

THE GALLERY

I stopped over at a motel on E3.
In my room was a smell that I knew from before
in a museum's Asiatic collections:

masks Tibetan Japanese against a light wall.

It isn't masks now but faces

that penetrate the white wall of forgetfulness
to breathe, to ask for something.
I lie awake and see them struggle
and disappear and return.

Some borrow each other's shapes, change faces
deep within me
where forgetfulness and memory go on with their bargaining.

They penetrate the painting-over of forgetfulness
the white wall
they disappear and return.

There is a sorrow here that doesn't call itself that.

Welcome to the real galleries!
Welcome to the real galleys!
The real gratings!

The karate boy who paralyzed a man
still dreams of fast profits.

This woman buys and buys things
to throw into the mouth of the empty space
that slinks behind her.

Mr. X doesn't dare leave his apartment.
A dark fence of ambiguous people
stands between him
and the horizon rolling steadily away.

She who once fled from Karelia
she who could laugh . . .
she appears now
but mute, turned to stone, a statue from Sumer.

As when I was ten years old and came home late.
In the stairway the lights were turned out.
But the elevator where I stood was lit, and the elevator
climbed like a diving bell through black depths
floor by floor while imagined faces
pressed against the grille.

But they are real faces now, not imagined ones.

I lie stretched out like a cross street.

Many climb out of the white mist.
We touched each other once, certainly!

A long light corridor that smells of carbolic acid.
The wheelchair. The teen-age girl
who is learning to talk after the car crash.

He who tried to call out under water
and the cold mass of the world squeezed in
through his nose and mouth.

Voices in the microphone said: Speed is power
speed is power!
Play the game, the show must go on!

In our careers we move stiffly step by step
as in a Noh play
with masks, shrieking song: Me, it's me!
The ones that lose out
are represented by a rolled-up blanket.

An artist said: Before, I was a planet
with its own thick atmosphere.
The rays from outside were broken up into rainbows,
continuous thunderstorms raged within, within.

Now I'm burned out and dry and open.
I don't have the energy of a child now.
I have a hot side and a cold side.

No rainbows.

I stopped over at the house where things could be heard.
Many want to come in there through the walls
but most don't find their way.

They are shouted down by the white noise of forgetfulness.

Anonymous song drowns in the walls.
Delicate knockings that don't want to be heard
drawn-out sighs
my old answers creeping homelessly.

Listen to society's mechanical self-reproaches
the large air conditioner's voice
like the artificial gale in the mine shafts
six hundred meters down.

Our eyes stay wide open under the bandage.

If I can at least get them to feel
that the shaking under us
means that we're on a bridge . . .

Often I have to stand completely motionless.
I'm the partner of the knife thrower in the circus!
Questions I threw from me in a fit of rage
come whining back
don't hit but nail down my shape
in coarse outline
stay there when I've left the place.

Often I have to remain silent. Willingly!
Because the "last word" is said again and again.
Because hello and good-bye . . .
Because a day like today . . .

Because the margins will finally rise
over their edges
and drown the text.

I stopped over at the sleepwalkers' hotel.
Many faces in here are desperate
others smoothed away
after their pilgrimage through forgetfulness.

They breathe disappear fight their way back
they see past me
they all want to go toward the icon of justice.

It happens, but seldom,
that one of us really sees the other:

a person shows himself a moment
as in a photo but clearer
and in the background
something that is bigger than his shadow.

He stands full length in front of a mountain.
It's more a snail shell than a mountain.
It's more a house than a snail shell.
It isn't a house but has many rooms.
It's indistinct but overwhelming.
He grows from it and it from him.
It is his life, it is his labyrinth.

BELOW FREEZING

We are at a party that doesn't love us. Finally the party lets the mask fall and shows what it is: a shunting station for freight cars. In the fog cold giants stand on their tracks. A scribble of chalk on the car doors.

One can't say it aloud, but there is a lot of repressed violence here. That is why the furnishings seem so heavy. And why it is so difficult to see the other thing present: a spot of sun that moves over the house walls and slips over the unaware forest of flickering faces, a biblical saying never set down: "Come unto me, for I am as full of contradictions as you."

I work the next morning in a different town. I drive there in a hum through the dawning hour which resembles a dark blue cylinder. Orion hangs over the frost. Children stand in a silent clump, waiting for the school bus, the children no one prays for. The light grows as gradually as our hair.

THE BLACK MOUNTAINS

At the next bend the bus broke free of the mountain's cold shadow,
turned its nose to the sun and crept roaring upwards.
We were packed in. The dictator's bust was there too,
wrapped in newspaper. A bottle passed from mouth to mouth.
Death, the birthmark, was growing on all of us, quicker on some, slower
    on others.
Up in the mountains the blue sea caught up with the sky.

HOMEWARDS

A telephone call ran out in the night and glittered over the countryside
and in the suburbs.
Afterwards I slept uneasily in the hotel bed.
I was like the needle in a compass carried through the forest by an orienteer
with a thumping heart.

A PART OF THE FOREST

On the way there a pair of frightened wings clattered up, that was all. There you walk alone. It's a high building completely made of narrow cracks. A building that is always swaying but never falls. The thousandfold sun slips in through the cracks. In the play of light an inverted law of gravity prevails: the house is anchored in the sky, and everything that falls falls upward. You can turn around there. You can mourn there. There you dare look at certain old truths that otherwise are always kept packed away. The parts I play deep within float up there, hang like dried skulls in the ancestors' hut on some remote Melanesian island. An atmosphere of childhood around the spooky trophies. It's so mild in the forest.

AT FUNCHAL

(Island of Madeira)

On the beach there's a seafood place, simple, a shack thrown up by survivors of the shipwreck. Many turn back at the door, but not the sea winds. A shadow stands deep inside his smoky hut frying two fish according to an old recipe from Atlantis, tiny garlic explosions, oil running over sliced tomatoes, every morsel says that the ocean wishes us well, a humming from the deep places.

She and I look into each other. It's like climbing the wild-flowered mountain slopes without feeling the least bit tired. We've sided with the animals, they welcome us, we don't age. But we have experienced so much together over the years, including those times when we weren't so good (as when we stood in line to give blood to the healthy giant—he said he wanted a transfusion), incidents which should have separated us if they hadn't united us, and incidents which we've totally forgotten—though they haven't forgotten us! They've turned to stones, dark and light, stones in a scattered mosaic. And now it happens: the pieces move towards each other, the mosaic appears and is whole. It waits for us. It glows down from the hotel-room wall, some figure violent and tender, perhaps a face, we can't take it all in as we pull off our clothes.

After dusk we go out. The dark powerful paw of the cape lies thrown out into the sea. We walk in swirls of human beings, we are cuffed around kindly, among soft tyrannies, everyone chatters excitedly in the foreign tongue. "No man is an island." We gain strength from *them,* but also from ourselves. From what is inside that the other person can't see. That which can only meet itself. The innermost paradox, the underground garage flowers, the vent towards the good dark. A drink that bubbles in empty glasses. An amplifier that magnifies silence. A path that grows over after every step. A book that can only be read in the dark.

9

FROM

*THE WILD MARKET
SQUARE (1983)*

BRIEF PAUSE IN THE
ORGAN RECITAL

The organ stops playing and it's deathly quiet in the church, but only for
    a couple of seconds.
And the faint rumbling penetrates from the traffic out there, that greater
    organ.

For we are surrounded by the murmuring of the traffic, it flows along the
    cathedral walls.
The outer world glides there like a transparent film and with shadows
    struggling pianissimo.

And as if it were part of the street noise I hear one of my pulses beating in
    the silence,
I hear my blood circulating, the cascade that hides inside me, that I walk
    about with

and as close as my blood and as far away as a memory from when I was four
I hear the trailer that rumbles past and makes the six-hundred-year-old
    walls tremble.

This could hardly be less like a mother's lap, yet at the moment I am a
    child,
hearing the grown-ups talking far away, the voices of the winners and the
    losers mingling.

On the blue benches a sparse congregation. And the pillars rise like strange
    trees:
no roots (only the common floor) and no crown (only the common roof).

I relive a dream. That I'm standing alone in a churchyard. Everywhere
    heather glows
as far as the eye can reach. Who am I waiting for? A friend. Why doesn't
    he come? He's here already.

Slowly death turns up the lights from underneath, from the ground. The
heath shines, a stronger and stronger purple—
no, a color no one has seen . . . until the morning's pale light whines in
through the eyelids

and I waken to that unshakable PERHAPS that carries me through the wav-
ering world.
And each abstract picture of the world is as impossible as the blueprint of
a storm.

At home stood the all-knowing Encyclopedia, a yard of bookshelf, in it I
learnt to read.
But each one of us has his own encyclopedia written, it grows out of each
soul,

it's written from birth onwards, the hundreds of thousands of pages stand
pressed against each other
and yet with air between them! Like the quivering leaves in a forest. The
book of contradictions.

What's there changes by the hour, the pictures retouch themselves, the
words flicker.
A wake washes through the whole text, it's followed by the next wave, and
then the next . . .

FROM MARCH '79

Tired of all who come with words, words but no language
I went to the snow-covered island.
The wild does not have words.
The unwritten pages spread themselves out in all directions!
I come across the marks of roe-deer's hooves in the snow.
Language but no words.

MEMORIES WATCH ME

A morning in June when it's too early yet
to wake, and still too late to go back to sleep.

I must go out through greenery that's crammed
with memories, that follow me with their eyes.

They are not visible, wholly dissolve
into background, perfect chameleons.

They are so close that I can hear them breathe
although the singing of birds is deafening.

THE WINTER'S GLANCE

Like a ladder I lean over and put
my face into the first floor of the cherry tree.
I am inside the bell of colors that rings with the sun.
I finish off the black-red cherries faster than four magpies.

Then suddenly I feel the chill from far off.
The moment blackens
and stays like the mark of the axe in the tree trunk.

From now on it's late. We go off half-running
out of sight, down, down into the antique sewer system.
The tunnels. We wander there for months
half out of duty and half in flight.

Brief devotions when some hatch opens above us
and a weak light falls.
We look upwards, the starry sky through the grating of the sewer.

THE STATION

A train has rolled in. Carriage after carriage stands,
but no doors open, no one gets off or on.
Are there no doors to be found at all? In there it is crowded
with locked-in people who are moving to and fro.
They are staring out through the immovable windows.
And outside a man goes along the train with a hammer.
He strikes on the wheels, which toll faintly. Except right here!
Here the ringing swells incomprehensibly: a thunderclap,
a cathedral-bells-sound, a world-circumnavigating-sound,
that lifts the whole train and the neighborhood's wet stones.
Everything is singing. You will remember this. Proceed!

ANSWERS TO LETTERS

In the bottom drawer of my desk I come across a letter that first arrived twenty-six years ago. A letter in panic, and it's still breathing when it arrives the second time.

A house has five windows: through four of them the day shines clear and still. The fifth faces a black sky, thunder and storm. I stand at the fifth window. The letter.

Sometimes an abyss opens between Tuesday and Wednesday but twenty-six years may be passed in a moment. Time is not a straight line, it's more of a labyrinth, and if you press close to the wall at the right place you can hear the hurrying steps and the voices, you can hear yourself walking past there on the other side.

Was the letter ever answered? I don't remember, it *was* long ago. The countless thresholds of the sea went on migrating. The heart went on leaping from second to second like the toad in the wet grass of an August night.

The unanswered letters pile up, like cirrostratus clouds presaging bad weather. They make the sunbeams lusterless. One day I will answer. One day when I am dead and can at last concentrate. Or at least so far away from here that I can find myself again. When I'm walking, newly arrived, in the big city, on 125th Street, in the wind on the street of dancing garbage. I who love to stray off and vanish in the crowd, a capital T in the mass of the endless text.

THE ICELANDIC HURRICANE

Not a shuddering of the earth but a skyquake. Turner could have painted it, firmly lashed down. A single glove whirled past just now, many kilometers from its hand. I shall make my way along against the wind to that house on the other side of the field. I am flickering in the hurricane. I am being X-rayed, my skeleton is handing in its resignation. Panic grows while I cross, I founder, I founder and drown on dry land! What a burden it is, all I have to drag along suddenly, what a burden for the butterfly to take a barge in tow! Arrived at last. A final wrestling with the door. And inside now. Inside now. Behind the big pane of glass. What a strange and magnificent idea glass is—to be close without being struck. . . . Outside a horde of transparent sprinters of gigantic shape is rushing by over the plateau of lava. But I no longer founder. I sit behind the glass, still, my own portrait.

THE BLUE WIND-FLOWERS

To be spellbound—nothing's easier. It's one of the oldest tricks of the soil and springtime: the blue wind-flowers. They are in a way unexpected. They shoot up out of the brown rustle of last year in overlooked places where one's gaze never pauses. They glimmer and float, yes, float, and that comes from their color. That sharp violet-blue now weighs nothing. Here is ecstasy, but low-voiced. "Career"—irrelevant! "Power" and "publicity"—ridiculous! They must have laid on a great reception up in Nineveh, with "pompe" and "Trompe up!" Raising the rafters. And above all those brows the crowning crystal chandeliers hung like glass vultures. Instead of such an overdecorated and strident cul-de-sac, the wind-flowers open a secret passage to the real celebration, which is quiet as death.

THE BLUE HOUSE

It is a night of radiant sun. I stand in the dense forest and look towards my house with its haze-blue walls. As if I had recently died and saw the house from a new angle.

It has stood more than eighty summers. Its wood is impregnated with four times joy and three times sorrow. When someone who lived in the house dies it is repainted. The dead person himself does the painting, without a brush, from within.

On the other side there is open terrain. Once a garden, now overgrown. Unmoving breakers of weeds, pagodas of weeds, pouring forth text, Upanishads of weeds, a Viking fleet of weeds, dragon heads, lances, an empire of weeds!

The shadow of a boomerang thrown over and over again flaps above the overgrown garden. It is connected with someone who lived in the house long before my time. Almost a child. An impulse issues from him, a thought, a command, "create . . . draw . . ." To be able to escape his fate.

The house looks like a child's drawing. A vicarious childishness that developed because someone too early abandoned the task of being a child. Open the door, come inside! Inside there is unrest in the ceiling and peace in the walls. Over the bed hangs an amateur painting of a ship with seventeen sails, hissing crests of the waves, and a wind that the gilded frame can't stop.

It is always so early inside here, before the fork in the road, before the irrevocable decision. Thanks for this life! Still, I miss alternatives. All sketches want to become real.

Far off over the water a motor stretches the summer night's horizon. Both joy and sorrow swell in the magnifying glass of the dew. We don't really know it, but we sense it: there is a sister ship to our life which takes a totally different route. While the sun burns behind the islands.

NINETEEN HUNDRED AND EIGHTY

He glances fitfully over the newspaper page.
Feelings come, so chilled they're taken for thoughts.
Only in deep hypnosis could he be his other I,
his hidden sister, the woman who goes with the hundred thousand
screaming "Death to the Shah!"—though he is already dead—
a marching black tent, pious and full of hate.
Jihad! Two who shall never meet take charge of the world.

BLACK POSTCARDS

I
The calendar full, future unknown.
The cable hums the folksong from no country.
Falling snow on the lead-still sea. Shadows
               wrestle on the dock.

II
In the middle of life it happens that death comes
and takes your measurements. This visit
is forgotten and life goes on. But the suit is
               sewn in the silence.

FIRESCRIBBLING

During the dismal months, my life sparkled only when I made love with
  you.
As the firefly ignites and then goes out, ignites, goes out—one can follow
  its flight by glimpses
in the dark night among the olive trees.

During the dismal months the soul sat shrunken and lifeless,
but the body took the straight path to you.
The night sky bellowed.
By stealth we milked the cosmos and survived.

POSTLUDIUM

I drag over the floor of the world like a grappling hook.
Everything I have no need of catches on it.
Tired indignation, glowing resignation.
The executioners gather stones, God writes in the sand.

Quiet rooms.
In the moonlight the furniture looks ready to bolt.
I walk slowly into myself
through a forest of empty armor.

DREAM SEMINAR

Four thousand million on earth.
They all sleep, they all dream.
Faces throng, and bodies, in each dream—
the dreamt-of people are more numerous
than us. But take no space . . .
You doze off at the theater perhaps,
in mid-play your eyelids sink.
A fleeting double exposure: the stage
before you outmaneuvered by a dream.
Then no more stage, it's you.
The theater in the honest depths!
The mystery of the overworked director!
Perpetual memorizing of new plays . . .
A bedroom. Night.
The darkened sky is flowing through the room.
The book that someone fell asleep from lies
still open
sprawling wounded at the edge of the bed.
The sleeper's eyes are moving,
they're following the text without letters
in another book—
illuminated, old-fashioned, swift.
A dizzying commedia inscribed
within the eyelids' monastery walls.
A unique copy. Here, this very moment.
In the morning, wiped out.
The mystery of the great waste!
Annihilation. As when suspicious men
in uniforms stop the tourist—
open his camera, unwind the film
and let the daylight kill the pictures:
thus dreams are blackened by the light of day.
Annihilated or just invisible?
There is a kind of out-of-sight dreaming

that never stops. Light for other eyes.
A zone where creeping thoughts learn to walk.
Faces and forms regrouped.
We're moving on a street, among people
in blazing sun.
But just as many—maybe more—
we don't see
are also there in dark buildings
high on both sides.
Sometimes one of them comes to the window
and glances down on us.

CODEX

The men of the footnotes, not the headlines . . . I find myself in the deep
  corridor
that would be dark
if my right hand weren't shining like a flashlight.
The light falls on something written on the wall
and I see it
the way the diver sees the name on the sunken hull flickering towards him
  in the streaming depth:
ADAM ILEBORGH 1448. Who?
The one who got the organ to stretch its clumsy wings and rise—
it kept itself hovering almost a minute.
What a successful experiment!
Written on the wall: MAYONE. DAUTHENDEY. KAMINSKI . . .
  The light falls on name after name.
The walls are covered with scribbles.
They are the almost rubbed-out names of the artists
the men of the footnotes, the unplayed, the half forgotten, the deathless
  unknowns.
For a moment it feels as if they all are whispering their names at the same
  time—
whisper upon whisper adding up to a breaker that rushes along the corridor
without knocking anyone over.
Besides, it isn't a corridor anymore.
Neither burial place nor market square but something of both.
It's also a greenhouse.
Here is plenty of oxygen.
The dead of the footnotes can breathe deeply, they are included in the
  ecological system just as before.
But they escape so much!
They escape swallowing the morality of power
they escape the black-and-white checkered game where the corpses' stench
  is the only thing that never dies.
They are rehabilitated.
And the ones that can't receive any more

haven't stopped giving.
They unrolled the glowing and melancholy tapestry a bit
and then loosened their grip.
Some are anonymous, they are my friends
but I don't recognize them. They are like those stone people
carved on grave slabs in old churches.
Mild or severe reliefs on walls that we brush against, figures and names
sunk into the stone floor, being rubbed away.
But the ones who really want to be taken off the list . . .
They don't stay in the territory of the footnotes
they go into a declining career that ends in oblivion and peace.
The total oblivion. It's a kind of examination
that is taken in silence, to walk across the border and no one notices . . .

CARILLON

Madame despises her guests because they want to stay at her shabby hotel.
I have the corner room, one floor up: a wretched bed, a light bulb in the ceiling.
Heavy drapes where a quarter of a million mites are on the march.

Outside, a pedestrian street
with slow tourists, hurrying schoolchildren, men in working clothes who wheel their rattling bikes.
Those who think they make the earth go round and those who think they go round helplessly in earth's grip.
A street we all walk, where does it emerge?

The room's only window faces something else: The Wild Market Square,
ground that seethes, a wide trembling surface, at times crowded and at times deserted.

What I carry within me is materialized there, all terrors, all expectations.
All the inconceivable that will nevertheless happen.

I have low beaches, if death rises six inches I shall be flooded.

I am Maximilian. It's 1488. I'm held prisoner here in Bruges
because my enemies are irresolute—
they are wicked idealists and what they did in horror's backyard I can't describe, I can't turn blood into ink.

I am also the man in overalls wheeling his rattling bike down on the street.
I am also the person seen, that tourist, the one loitering and pausing, loitering and pausing
and letting his gaze wander over the pale moontanned faces and surging draperies of the old paintings.

No one decides where I go, least of all myself, though each step is where it must be.

Walking round in the fossil-wars where all are invulnerable because all are dead!

The dusty foliage, the walls with their loopholes, the garden paths where petrified tears crunch under the heels . . .

Unexpectedly, as if I'd stepped on a trip-wire, the bell-ringing starts in the anonymous tower.
Carillon! The sack splits along its seams and the chimes roll out across Flanders.
Carillon! The cooing iron of the bells, hymn and hit song in one, and tremblingly written in the air.
The shaky-handed doctor wrote out a prescription that no one can decipher but his writing will be recognized . . .

Over meadow and housetop, harvest and mart,
over the quick and the dead the carillon rings.
Christ and Antichrist, hard to tell them apart!
The bells bear us home at last on their wings.

. They have stopped.

I am back in the hotel room: the bed, the light, the drapes. There are strange noises, the cellar is dragging itself up the stairs.

I lie on the bed with my arms outstretched.
I am an anchor that has dug itself down and holds steady
the huge shadow floating up there,
the great unknown which I am a part of and which is certainly more important than me.

Outside, the walkway, the street where my steps die away and also what is written, my preface to silence and my inside-out psalm.

MOLOKAI

We stand at the edge of the cliff and in the depths beneath us gleam the
    roofs of the leper colony.
We could climb down, but we don't have time to make it back before
    dark.
So we turn back through the forest, walk among trees with long blue needles.
It is still. It is the stillness when the hawk comes.
It is a forest that forgives everything but forgets nothing.
Damien, out of love, chose life and oblivion. He found death and fame.
But we see these events from the wrong angle: a heap of stones instead of
    the face of the sphinx.

10

NEW POEMS

STREETS IN SHANGHAI

I
Many in the park are reading the white butterfly.
I love that cabbage butterfly as if it were a fluttering corner of truth itself!

At dawn the running crowds set our silent planet going.
Then the park fills with people. For each one eight faces polished like jade,
   for all situations, to avoid mistakes.
For each one also the invisible face that reflects "something you don't talk
   about."
Something that emerges in tired moments and is as pungent as a sip of
   Viper schnapps, with its long, scaly aftertaste.

The carp in the pond are always moving, they swim while they're sleeping,
   they are an example for the faithful: always in motion.

II
Now it's noon. The washing flutters in the gray sea wind high above the
   cyclists
who come in tight shoals. Notice the labyrinths to the sides!

I am surrounded by written characters I can't interpret. I am illiterate
   through and through.
But I have paid what I'm supposed to and I have receipts for everything. I
   have gathered so many unreadable receipts.
I am an old tree with withered leaves that hang on and can't fall to earth.

And a gust from the sea rustles all these receipts.

III
At dawn the trudging crowds set our silent planet going.
We're all on board the street, it's as crowded as the deck of a ferry.
Where are we going? Are there enough teacups? We can consider ourselves
   fortunate for getting on this street in time!
It's a thousand years before the birth of claustrophobia.

Behind each one walking here hovers a cross that wants to catch up to us, pass us, join us.
Something that wants to sneak up on us from behind and cover our eyes and whisper, "Guess who?"

We look almost happy out in the sun, while we bleed to death from wounds we know nothing about.

THE FORGOTTEN CAPTAIN

We have many shadows. I was walking home
in the September night when Y
climbed out of his grave after forty years
and kept me company.

At first he was quite empty, only a name
but his thoughts swam
faster than time ran
and caught up with us.

I put his eyes to my eyes
and saw war's ocean.
The last boat he captained
took shape beneath us.

Ahead and astern the Atlantic convoy crept,
the ships that would survive
and the ships that bore the Mark
(invisible to all)

while sleepless days relieved each other
but never him.
Under his oilskin, his life-jacket.
He never came home.

It was an internal weeping that bled him to death
in a Cardiff hospital,
he could at last lie down
and turn into a horizon.

Good-bye, eleven-knot convoys! Good-bye, 1940!
Here ends world history.
The bombers were left hanging.
The heathery moors blossomed.

A photo from early this century shows a beach.
Six Sunday-best boys.
Sailing-boats in their arms.
What solemn airs!

The boats that became life and death for some of them.
And writing about the dead—
that too is a game made heavy
with what is to come.

THE NIGHTINGALE IN
BADELUNDA

In the green midnight at the nightingale's northern limit. Heavy leaves
hang in trance, the deaf cars race towards the neon-line. The nightingale's
voice rises without wavering to the side, it is as penetrating as a cock-crow,
but beautiful and free of vanity. I was in prison and it visited me. I was
sick and it visited me. I didn't notice it then, but I do now. Time streams
down from the sun and the moon and into all the tick-tock-thankful clocks.
But right here there is no time. Only the nightingale's voice, the raw
resonant notes that whet the night sky's gleaming scythe.

VERMEER

No sheltered world . . . on the other side of the wall the noise begins
the tavern begins
with laughter and bickering, rows of teeth, tears, the din of bells
and the mentally disordered brother-in-law, the bearer of death that everyone
    must tremble for.

The great explosion and the delayed tramp of rescuers
the boats that strut at anchor, the money that creeps into the pocket of the
    wrong person
demands piled on demands
Cusps of gaping red flowers that sweat premonitions of war.

Away from there and straight through the wall into the bright studio
into the second that goes on living for hundreds of years.
Paintings titled *The Music Lesson*
or *Woman in Blue Reading a Letter*—
she's in her eighth month, two hearts kicking inside her.
On the wall behind her hangs a wrinkled map of Terra Incognita.

Breathes calmly . . . An unknown blue material is nailed to the chair.
The gold upholstery tacks flew in with unheard-of speed
and stopped abruptly
as if they had never been anything but stillness.

The ears ring with either depth or height.
It's the pressure from the other side of the wall
that leaves every fact suspended
and holds the brush steady.

It hurts to go through walls, it makes you sick
but it's necessary.
The world is one. But walls . . .
And the wall is part of yourself—

Whether you know it or not it's the same for everyone,
everyone except little children. No walls for them.

The clear sky has set itself on a slant against the wall.
It's like a prayer to emptiness.
And the emptiness turns its face to us
and whispers,
"I am not empty, I am open."